OUT-OF-THE-BOX LEADERSHIP

The Soul of Educational Leadership

Alan M. Blankstein, Paul D. Houston, Robert W. Cole, Editors

THE SOUL OF EDUCATIONAL LEADERSHIP

OUT-OF-THE-BOX LEADERSHIP

PAUL D. HOUSTON ⁊ ALAN M. BLANKSTEIN ⁊ ROBERT W. COLE

EDITORS

A JOINT PUBLICATION

CORWIN PRESS

HOPE Foundation

American Association of
School Administrators

CORWIN PRESS
A SAGE Publications Company
Thousand Oaks, CA 91320

For information:

Corwin Press
A Sage Publications Company
2455 Teller Road
Thousand Oaks, California 91320
www.corwinpress.com

Sage Publications Ltd.
1 Oliver's Yard
55 City Road
London EC1Y 1SP
United Kingdom

Sage Publications India Pvt. Ltd.
B-42, Panchsheel Enclave
Post Box 4109
New Delhi 110 017   India

Printed in the United States of America

Library of Congress Cataloging-in-Publication Data

Out-of-the-box leadership/[edited by] Paul D. Houston, Alan M. Blankstein, Robert W. Cole.
    p. cm.—(The soul of educational leadership series; v.2)
    "A joint publication with the Hope Foundation, The National Association of Elementary School Principals, and the American Association of School Administrators."
Includes index.
ISBN 978-1-4129-3845-7 (cloth)—ISBN 978-1-4129-3846-4 (pbk.)
    1. School management and organization. 2. Educational leadership. 3. Leadership.
I. Houston, Paul D. II. Blankstein, Alan M., 1959- III. Cole, Robert W., 1945-
IV. Hope Foundation. V. Title. VI. Series.

LB2805.O767 2007
371.2—dc22   2006035774

This book is printed on acid-free paper.

07   08   09   10   11   10 9 8 7 6 5 4 3 2

Acquisitions Editor:	Elizabeth Brenkus
Editorial Assistant:	Desirée Enayati
Production Editor:	Libby Larson
Copy Editor:	Teresa Herlinger
Typesetter:	C&M Digitals (P) Ltd.
Proofreader:	Word Wise Webb
Indexer:	Nara Wood
Cover Designer:	Michael Dubowe

CONTENTS

ACKNOWLEDGMENTS

W e wish to express our gratitude to those Corwin Press staff members who served as our lifeline on this entire project: Faye Zucker and Lizzie Brenkus, our superb editors; Gem Rabanera and Desirée Enayati, their delightful, punctilious editorial assistants; Astrid Virding, who coordinated the painstaking task of turning a book's worth of manuscripts into a book; and Teresa Herlinger, who caught all the mistakes the rest of us missed. Without their unfailingly patient, knowledgeable work, there would be no *Soul of Educational Leadership* series. All of us are in their debt.

Corwin Press gratefully acknowledges the contributions of the following individuals:

Chuck Bonner, Assistant Principal
Great Valley High School
Malvern, PA

Kermit Buckner, Professor
Dept. of Educational Leadership
East Carolina University
Greenville, NC

Shelby Cosner, Assistant Professor
University of Illinois at Chicago
Chicago, IL

Kenneth Killian, Assistant Professor
School of Education
Vanguard University of Southern California
Costa Mesa, CA

Guylene Robertson, Assistant Superintendent
Cleveland Independent School District
Cleveland, TX

Paul Young, Executive Director
West After School Center, Inc.
Lancaster, OH

ABOUT THE EDITORS

Paul D. Houston has served as executive director of the American Association of School Administrators since 1994.

Dr. Houston has established himself as one of the leading spokespersons for American education through his extensive speaking engagements, published articles, and his regular appearances on national radio and television.

Dr. Houston served previously as a teacher and building administrator in North Carolina and New Jersey. He has also served as assistant superintendent in Birmingham, Alabama, and as superintendent of schools in Princeton, New Jersey; Tucson, Arizona; and Riverside, California.

Dr. Houston has also served in an adjunct capacity for the University of North Carolina, Harvard University, Brigham Young University, and Princeton University. He has served as a consultant and speaker throughout the United States and overseas, and he has published more than 100 articles in professional journals.

Alan M. Blankstein is founder and president of the HOPE Foundation, a not-for-profit organization whose honorary chair is Nobel Prize winner Archbishop Desmond Tutu. The HOPE Foundation (Harnessing Optimism and Potential through Education) is dedicated to supporting educational leaders over time in creating school cultures where failure is not an option for any student. HOPE sustains student success.

The HOPE Foundation brought W. Edwards Deming and his work to light in educational circles, beginning with the Shaping Chicago's Future conference in 1988. From 1988 to 1992, in a series of Shaping America's Future forums and PBS video conferences, he brought together scores of national and world leaders including

Al Shanker; Peter Senge; Mary Futrell; Linda Darling-Hammond; Ed Zigler; and CEO's of GM, Ford, and other corporations to determine how best to bring quality concepts and those of "learning organizations" to bear in educational systems.

The HOPE Foundation provides professional development for thousands of educational leaders annually throughout North America and other parts of the world, including South Africa. HOPE also provides long-term support for school improvement through leadership academies and intensive on-site school change efforts, leading to dramatic increases in student achievement in diverse settings.

A former "high risk" youth, Alan began his career in education as a music teacher and has worked within youth-serving organizations for 20 years, including the March of Dimes, Phi Delta Kappa, and the National Educational Service (NES), which he founded in 1987 and directed for 12 years.

He coauthored with Rick DuFour the *Reaching Today's Youth* curriculum, now provided as a course in 16 states, and has contributed writing to *Educational Leadership, The School Administrator, Executive Educator, High School Magazine, Reaching Today's Youth,* and *EQ + IQ = Best Leadership Practices for Caring and Successful Schools.* Alan has provided keynote presentations and workshops for virtually every major educational organization. He is author of the best-selling book *Failure Is Not an Option™: Six Principles That Guide Student Achievement in High-Performing Schools,* which has been awarded "Book of the Year" by the National Staff Development Council, and nominated for three other national and international awards.

Alan is on the Harvard International Principals Center's advisory board, has served as a board member for the Federation of Families for Children's Mental Health, is a cochair of Indiana University's Neal Marshall Black Culture Center's Community Network, and is advisor to the Faculty and Staff for Student Excellence mentoring program. Alan is also an advisory board member for the Forum on Race, Equity, and Human Understanding with the Monroe County Schools in Indian, and has served on the Board of Trustees for the Jewish Child Care Agency (JCCA), at which he was once a youth-in-residence.

Robert W. Cole, proprietor of Edu-Data, is a writer, editor, and consultant in Louisville, Kentucky. His credentials include 14 years at *Phi Delta Kappan* magazine, 7 of them as editor-in-chief; 10 years as president of the Educational Press Association of America and member of the Ed Press Board of Directors; 4 years as founding vice president of the Schlechty Center for Leadership in School Reform; 11 years as senior consultant to the National Reading Styles Institute; and book development editor for the Association for Supervision and Curriculum Development (ASCD) and for The Writer's Edge Press, where he currently serves as chief creative consultant. Bob is editor and lead writer of the two-volume, best-selling ASCD book *Educating Everybody's Children*. He has presented workshops, master classes, and lectures at universities nationwide, including Harvard, Stanford, and Indiana Universities, as well as serving as special consultant to college and university deans in working with faculties on writing for professional publication.

ABOUT THE CONTRIBUTORS

Kari Cocozzella has been a principal for eight years in the Adams 12 Five-Star District in the north metropolitan area of Denver. Her stories come from experiences as a leader in two schools, Skyview Elementary and Coyote Ridge Elementary. Even though both schools are in the same district, the needs of each school presented different challenges and opportunities. Kari's commitment to professional learning communities and building leadership capacity in others is paramount in her daily actions and interactions with the school and community.

Thomas J. Kasper is currently the principal at Dakota Valley in Cherry Creek Schools, a large suburban district located in the Denver metropolitan area. After serving as an administrator in Grand Junction, Colorado, the previous nine years, during which he explored and implemented the concepts of professional learning communities, organizational learning, and the precepts of effective leadership, he chose to deepen his own learning by deliberately removing himself from the known and moving into the unknown. Because of this, Tom has been able to model the significance of being both a teacher and a learner in his role as a school leader.

Jane A. Kendrick is the assistant superintendent for high school education for the Indianapolis Public Schools. She is responsible for the education of 12,000 students, oversees seven high school campuses and the implementation of 23 small high schools, and serves as the district's liaison to the Bill and Melinda Gates Foundation for high school transformation. She has served as president of the Indiana Urban Schools Association, and served for over 20 years as a principal and school superintendent in Indiana. Kendrick's work as a school principal was highlighted in Thomas J. Sergiovanni's book

Value-Added Leadership (1988). Kendrick has devoted her career to advancing educational equity and opportunity for urban youth. She received her EdD in educational administration from the University of Illinois at Urbana-Champaign.

Jerome T. Murphy is a specialist in the management and politics of education. His teaching and research focus on administrative practice and organizational leadership, government policy, program implementation and evaluation, and qualitative methodology. He has examined educational policy and practices in England, Australia, Colombia, China, and South Africa, and has participated in international exchange meetings on educational issues in Denmark, Sweden, Norway, Israel, and Russia. Murphy also conducted some of the earliest studies of the implementation of the Great Society education programs and the role of the states in educational policy and governance, and made substantial contributions to data-collection techniques in educational evaluation. More recently, he has written about the unheroic aspects of leadership in education, and about the changing roles of superintendents. For almost 20 years, Murphy was a full-time administrator at the Harvard Graduate School of Education, first as an associate dean from 1982 to 1991 and then as dean from 1992 to 2001. As dean, Murphy led the development of new initiatives in learning technologies, arts education, neuroscience and education, and school leadership. A former math teacher, he helped develop domestic legislation in the former U.S. Department of Health, Education, and Welfare; was associate director of the White House Fellows Program; and founded and directed the Massachusetts Internships in Education.

Les M. Omotani serves as superintendent for Hewlett-Woodmere Public Schools in Nassau County, Long Island, New York. He received his PhD from Iowa State University and is a past president of the ISU Alumni Association. He has taught at all grade levels including undergraduate and graduate students.

Les is a member of the Suburban School Superintendents of America. He is also a former member of the AASA National Advisory Council, the Danforth Forum for American School Superintendents, and the national advisory boards for the Grammy Foundation and IBM. He has participated and collaborated with Xerox in their quality tools and professional practice training.

During the past 15 years, Les has extensively collaborated with Dr. Peter Senge of MIT and his associates with the Society for Organizational Learning.

Les Omotani has a simple life's mission statement: "He cared and he served!"

Hank Rubin is joint dean of education at the University of South Dakota and South Dakota State University, the first dean of two independent public institutions in the nation. As this book goes to press, Dr. Rubin is assuming the position of dean of education and the Robert and Mildred Peronia Naslund Chair in the School of Education at the University of Redlands, California.

Rubin—who earned his PhD at Northwestern University and his MA and BA from the University of Chicago—served as associate superintendent for students, families, and communities for the State of Ohio; VP for sales and marketing for an international manufacturing firm; executive of several nonprofit agencies including the Institute for Collaborative Leadership, Citizens Schools Committee and the Institute for Voluntary Organizations; and has been a consultant and public speaker for hundreds of nonprofit, human service, education, and government agencies for over 25 years.

Rubin's articles and books examining public leadership, education policy and practice, social ethics, and philanthropy include *Collaborative Leadership: Developing Effective Partnerships in Communities and Schools* (Corwin Press, 2002); scholarly articles; and commentaries in *Education Week*, *The Chronicle of Higher Education*, and the *New York Times*.

Dennis Sparks has been executive director of the 10,000-member National Staff Development Council since 1984. Before this position, he was an independent educational consultant and director of the Northwest Staff Development Center (NSDC), a state and federally funded teacher center in Livonia, Michigan.

Dr. Sparks has also been a teacher, counselor, and codirector of an alternative high school. He completed his PhD in counseling at the University of Michigan in 1976. He speaks frequently throughout North America on topics such as powerful staff development and school leadership.

He is author of *Designing Powerful Professional Development for Teachers and Principals* (NSDC, 2002); *Conversations That Matter*

(NSDC, 2001), a collection of his *Journal of Staff Development* interviews since 1991; coauthor with Stephanie Hirsh of *Learning to Lead, Leading to Learn* (NSDC, 2000); coauthor with Joan Richardson, *What Is Staff Development Anyway?* (NSDC, 1998); and coauthor with Stephanie Hirsh, *A New Vision for Staff Development* (ASCD/NSDC, 1997).

Dr. Sparks's column appears each month in the newsletter *The Learning Principal,* a publication of the National Staff Development Council. In addition, his articles have appeared in a variety of publications, including *Educational Leadership, Phi Delta Kappan, The American School Board Journal, The Principal,* and *The School Administrator.*

All of Dr. Sparks's articles and interviews with educational leaders are accessible on the NSDC Web site at www.nsdc.org/library/authors/sparks.cfm

Thomas J. Sergiovanni is Lillian Radford Professor of Education at Trinity University, San Antonio, Texas, where he teaches in the school leadership program and in the five-year teacher education program. Sergiovanni received his master's degree from Teachers College, Columbia University, and his EdD in educational administration from the University of Rochester. He serves on the editorial boards of *Journal of Personnel Evaluation in Education, Catholic Education: A Journal of Inquiry and Practice, Journal of Research in Professional Learning,* and *Schools: Studies in Education.* Sergiovanni's recent books include *Moral Leadership* (1992), *Building Community in Schools* (1994), *Leadership for the Schoolhouse* (1996), *The Lifeworld of Leadership: Creating Culture, Community, and Personal Meaning in Our Schools* (2000), *Supervision: A Redefinition* (2002), and *Strengthening the Heartbeat: Leading and Learning Together in Schools* (2005). Sergiovanni holds honorary degrees from the State University of New York and the University of San Diego.

PREFACE

ROBERT W. COLE

W orking for the good of children is surely a vocation, a call-ing—not just a job. Like any calling, the work of education has both unique rewards and trying sacrifices. The nature of education—leading young people, readying them for life—calls on the hearts, the minds, and the souls of those who work within the schoolhouse doors. Thus the title of this multi-volume series: *The Soul of Educational Leadership.*

The initial volume, *Engaging EVERY Learner,* was selected to send a signal of all-inclusiveness. Every student matters deeply, to all of us in schools and in our society. Subsequent volumes feature contributions by leading thinkers and practitioners in the field on the soul-work of educational leadership. The overarching theme in Volume 1 was sounded by Alan Blankstein—editor of this series, together with myself and Paul Houston: "Saving young people from failure in school is equivalent to saving their lives!" Those powerful words set the tone for all that we hope to do in this series: "It is not easy or simple work, yet it can be done." And more, too: We know how to do what must be done.

In this second volume, *Out-of-the-Box Leadership,* Paul Houston sets the tone by observing that schools have been making incremental progress in an exponential environment: "We have grad-ually been improving education while the deteriorating social condi-tions surrounding families and children have confronted us with all sorts of new challenges." The executive director of the American Association of School Administrators (AASA), Houston calls for transformative leadership, which can come only by thinking differ-ently about our problems. Unfortunately, he notes, there aren't places to learn how to escape the boxes we've created. Helping educators and educational leaders escape their boxes is the primary purpose of this volume.

"Outside-the-box leaders create clarity out of confusion, optimism and efficacy out of resignation, and interdependence out of dependence," writes another executive director, Dennis Sparks, head of the National Staff Development Council, in his chapter, "What It Means to Be an Outside-the-Box Leader." High-quality leadership development is one of a school system's most important responsibilities, Sparks maintains, and he details the characteristics of such developmental work.

"To lead outside of the box, one must learn to think outside of the box!" claims Les Omotani, superintendent of the Hewlett-Woodmere Public Schools in Nassau County, Long Island, New York. "When we simply react to issues, we tend to see everything as a management problem to be solved," Omotani writes in "Caring, Serving . . . Leading." "When we focus on a shared vision, and the desired culture for our schools and community, we open the door for leadership."

In "An Epistemological Problem: What if We Have the Wrong Theory?" Thomas Sergiovanni, Lillian Radford Distinguished Professor at Trinity University in Houston, Texas, strikes a sobering note: "Improving schools is not as easy as it sounds. Hanging onto improvements once they are in place is even more difficult." What if we are using the wrong theories of leadership and of school improvement? "Developing new and more effective leadership designs and school improvement strategies requires making deeply rooted changes that result in breaking away from existing values and ideas."

"Reflections on Leadership: When Minds and Hearts Are Open," is framed as a coffee-shop discussion between Kari Cocozzella, an elementary principal in the Adams 12 Five-Star District, and Thomas J. Kasper, principal of Dakota Valley Elementary School in Cherry Creek Schools—both in metropolitan Denver. "Leaders must also be learners," they agree. "Having the courage to trust others enables a leader to recognize and access the best in everyone, including oneself. It's about *being* a leader rather than *doing* leadership; leadership is rooted in our humanity, not in a checklist of things to do."

Jane Kendrick has been principal of an urban middle school, superintendent of a PreK–12 urban school district, and consultant for strategic professional development to a large-city school district. In "Out-of-the-Box Leadership: A Reflection on Leading Educational

Transformation," she puts those pieces together, while noting sagely, "Promoting and engaging in out-of-the-box leadership should in no way negate the importance and purpose of continuing to engage in some in-the-box leadership."

Hank Rubin, formerly Joint Dean of Education at the University of South Dakota and South Dakota State University, recently assumed the position of Dean of Education and Robert & Mildred Peronia Naslund Chair in the School of Education at the University of Redlands, California. The lesson he's learned about leadership is this: "that it's fundamental to effective leadership to understand that not one of us leads programs, units, school sites, institutions, or district bureaucracies. Each one of us leads people—and we lead them in and through relationships." With this in mind, Rubin proposes a unifying theory or model that might guide practice, teaching, and professional development.

In the concluding chapter, Jerome Murphy, in "Embracing the Enemy: Moving Beyond the Pain of Leadership," dares to address the dark side of being a leader: pain. Murphy, Harold Howe II Professor of Education and former dean of the Harvard Graduate School of Education, writes, "Unlike the other authors in this volume, my goal is not to think 'outside the box' of leadership, but rather to shine a light inside the box—in this case, the Pandora's box that holds the inner struggles and personal demons of senior managers."

In this second volume of an eight-volume endeavor, we have enlisted some of the very best thinkers and doers we know to examine all sides of the enormously complex box that is American education—and even to peer into the dark heart that is our own fear of leading the charge, and failing. As Jerry Murphy wrote, "Ultimately, it's about moving forward on our journey—in work, in life, and in leadership." Once again, it is our aim to help strengthen you for this task.

CHAPTER ONE

OUT-OF-THE-BOX LEADERSHIP

PAUL D. HOUSTON

W e hear the phrase "getting out of the box" a lot, but what does it mean and why should we bother? After all, boxes are very useful. They keep our lives from getting all cluttered by giving us a place to put things. If you are a dog, they are a great spot for a nap. If you are a cat, well, you know the rest.

The problem arises if you are a leader. Leaders can't let themselves get boxed into old ways of thinking and being. Simply having a place to put old ways of doing, and finding comfort in that, is not enough. New challenges require new solutions, and even old challenges can only be overcome by taking a fresh look at them. It might be argued that finding ways to crawl out of the box has become a basic skill for leaders.

My friend Dawna Markova once said that we become the stories we tell ourselves. If one tells what she calls "rut stories," one becomes trapped in old ways of thinking and doing. Rut stories travel down well-worn neural pathways; they remind us of what we can't do and can't become. Dawna suggests that we consider another set of stories—what she calls "river stories." River stories take us to new places, but they can be scary because they take us to the unknown.

For many years, I have had a thing about bridges. I don't like driving over them. My palms get sweaty, and I clench the steering wheel tighter than a child holding a Popsicle. I once described this to a friend, who suggested that I had a "phobia" about bridges. I did not, I protested, because phobias are irrational fears, and there is nothing irrational about being afraid of bridges. Bridges take us from what we know to what we don't know—from a place that is familiar and safe to someplace that may be less safe.

And yet that is exactly the role of education and leadership. The role of an educational leader is to build a bridge and lead people across it, because it is only by crossing that bridge that people can find a new place to stand. Leading people to discover their river stories, and helping them build their bridges, is at the heart of leadership. But that can only happen when the leader is prepared to climb out of the familiar box that has held him or her and be willing to confront the possibility of the unknown.

> *The role of an educational leader is to build a bridge and lead people across it, because it is only by crossing that bridge that people can find a new place to stand.*

The problem is that there aren't places to learn how to get out of the box. It requires that one push one's own limits and perspectives. It involves changing the lens and the angle of vision. Cognitive scientists describe this as "lateral thinking." Lateral thinking involves consciously changing your mental seat to get a different view of the action. Lateral thinking is searching for related things in apparently unrelated activities. It is forging new paths to old places and taking old modes of transportation to new destinations.

I used to enjoy the comedian Jonathan Winters. His act involved using a simple item as a prop and then making up different stories, with the same item becoming a different thing with each story. Lateral thinking. Today's world requires us all to become Jonathan Winters, making the familiar new and the known fresh. That is out-of-the-box leadership.

Today we find education stuck in place. Oh, certainly some progress has been made. Schools today are superior to any in our history. Yet there has never been more dissatisfaction with schools. Quite simply, the problem is this: *Schools have been making incremental progress in an exponential environment.* We have gradually been improving education while the deteriorating social conditions surrounding families and children have confronted us with all sorts of new challenges, and the escalating demands of society and the workplace have forced upon education a much higher expectation.

Therefore, if we continue to improve the way we have, in a few years we'll be even better than we are today—and further behind. This calls for transformative leadership, and that can only come by thinking differently about our problems. As an exercise in out-of-the-box thinking, let me raise one

Quite simply, the problem is this: Schools have been making incremental progress in an exponential environment.

example that might illustrate how we must begin to think. It involves the concern over our international competitive position and what we should be doing about it educationally.

During the last few years, we have developed a growing concern about our global competitiveness, particularly in relation to the rising powers of India and China. This is similar to concerns in the 1980s about Japan and Germany, but this time the competition looms larger and the stakes are higher. This topic has been in the news, bandied about by CEOs and governors; it was a centerpiece of President Bush's 2006 State of the Union address. The hysteria could best be described as "the Asians are coming, the Asians are coming." And there is no doubt that the ascendance of China as an economic power and India as a place where many U.S. jobs go to die are legitimately raising concerns. Thomas Friedman, author of the best-selling book, *The World Is Flat,*[1] makes the case persuasively. Friedman suggests that, with the ascendance of China and India, the United States will have to run faster just to stay in place.

Today, hardly a CEO can be found who does not look with awe and concern at what is happening on the other side of the world. Many U.S. businesses have shipped jobs to both India and China. As with every previous threat to U.S. dominance, U.S. schools have been called to account for not producing enough engineers and math and science workers to compete with this rising threat. The educational solutions offered are that we should make our students work harder and study more math and science. Moreover, it is thought that we need more and harder tests to motivate them to do this.

The problem with the current thinking is that the problem just isn't that simple. First, the math doesn't add up for the United States.

Both India and China are massive countries. They need only to educate their elites and they would still have a gigantic edge in available knowledge workers. In the United States, we could make all our children high-tech workers and we would still be outnumbered. Furthermore, an engineer in either India or China will work for a fraction of the wages of his or her U.S. counterpart. To remain competitive, our workers would have to take monumental pay cuts and reductions in lifestyle simply to hold their own with Beijing and Bangalore. Left at this point, despair seems the only rational response.

The good news is that there is more to the story. Put most simply, the United States should compete at what it has always done best: being the innovative engine that drives the rest of the world economy. To do that, of course, will require increased efforts at producing more highly talented engineers and technical workers. To accomplish this, we must improve the way we teach math and science by making these subjects more engaging to students.

— ❦ —

The United States should compete at what it has always done best: being the innovative engine that drives the rest of the world economy.

But there is a larger issue emerging. Daniel Pink, in his provocative book *A Whole New Mind*,[2] has gone so far as to declare that the Information Age is nearing an end and that we are entering the Conceptual Age. He argues that the dominance of our left-brain–driven world, where everything is sequential and logical, is giving way to a more right-brained society that focuses on creative, holistic skills.

Pink suggests that if you have a job that can be done by a machine, done more cheaply, or done somewhere else, you have cause to worry. Those who do conceptual and creative work—design, storytelling, and the like—will dominate in this new age. Pink turns the current discussion upside down. It isn't about how many engineers a nation has; it's about the artists and poets who can create the new meaning necessary in a conceptual world.

Richard Florida, in his *Rise of the Creative Class*,[3] makes essentially the same argument. The future belongs to the creative. They will be the leaders, the learners, and the earners of the new age. It is not the programmers in India who will dominate; it is the people who conceive of the work the programmers should do who will "rule." Already we know that most of the places where the United States has an economic edge are those where our creative workers have gone before.

For example, our popular culture, best exemplified by the entertainment industry, is a major export for us; in fact, one might argue that "the American century," as some called the last century, came about not simply because of our economic or military might, but because we were the source of the images and sounds savored by people around the globe. Even our high-tech industries have found their dominance at the edge of this work creating new concepts of the way work should be done, or "imagineering" (as Disney calls it) new ways of doing things. Although it is important that our children be educated to be conversant and comfortable with math and science, and though we certainly need to continue to produce our fair share of technical workers, the future will not be created by these folks—it will be created by those who can dream bigger and more innovative dreams.

The implications for education are profound. We must reexamine how we are teaching children and what we are teaching them. I was one of those students who grew up hating math and science. I wasn't much happier with social studies and language arts. As an adult educator, I finally came to understand why. When I became superintendent of schools in Princeton, New Jersey, I was thrown into an environment rife with Nobel laureates and world-class theoretical mathematicians and physicists. Talking with them, I made a profound discovery. I found that the math I learned in school had the same relationship to mathematics as a log has to a blueberry.

> *We must reexamine how we are teaching children and what we are teaching them.*

Mathematics isn't about mastering rules; it is about discovering the *elegance* of a well-stated problem. And science is not about mastering element tables and formulas; it is about seeking out the *mysteries* of the universe. Likewise, social studies isn't about dates and events; it is about *understanding the human condition*. And literature is a way of coming to *understand* more about *ourselves*.

If we expect our children to become more adept at all these subjects, we must begin to educate our teachers to be more creative in the way the material is presented, as well as more knowledgeable about their subject matter. Teachers must be *designers* and *storytellers*. They have to get out of the box! Moreover, school leaders must reassess their roles as instructional leaders. How do we reinvent the learning process so it is meaningful and engaging for students, so they are motivated by more than a test or benchmark?

As one student said, quoted in a recent cover story in *Time* magazine on the current science crisis, "I associated engineering with long, boring assignments. No one showed me why it was cool."[4]

———————— ✥ ————————

How do we reinvent the learning process so it is meaningful and engaging for students, so they are motivated by more than a test or benchmark?

We must find a way to make learning relevant and "cool." We can only do that by having teachers who are supported in their creativity. The question becomes, How can we recruit and support teachers who see themselves as artists?

Sadly, the way we are currently approaching schooling in the United States, we are destined to become a third-rate economy and a Third World power. That is because we are forfeiting our greatest edge by walking away from what we do best. In a recent commentary in *Newsweek* magazine, Fareed Zakaria, editor of *Newsweek International,* described his conversations with various people in Asia about education.[5] China has increased their spending on colleges and universities tenfold in the past decade. This comes at a time when U.S. states, which cut taxes during the boom years of the1990s, are now struggling to hold their own in education spending, and when the recently proposed federal budget reduces support for education by more than $12 billion. Clearly it will be hard to maintain our edge without investment. Again, the recent story in *Time* magazine pointed out that the United States has slowed its investment in research and development at the very time that other countries have accelerated theirs. The United States currently ranks seventh in percentage of GDP spent on research.

But money is not the only issue. Zakaria talked with the minister of education in Singapore, a city-state whose education system is often compared to that of the United States. Singapore is the top-ranked performer on science and math global rankings for schoolchildren. Zakaria asked the minister to explain why it is that even though the Singaporean students do so well on these tests, when you look at the same students 10 to 20 years later, few are world-beaters. U.S. students, by contrast, test much worse but seem to do better in life and in the real world—particularly as inventors and entrepreneurs.

The minister explained that both countries have meritocracies— America's, based on talent; Singapore's, on test scores. Since there is much to the intellect that we cannot test effectively—such as creativity, curiosity, ambition, or a sense of adventure—the tests don't account for America's edge. The minister went on to explain that America's culture of learning challenges conventional wisdom, even to the point of challenging authority. He also suggested that these are the areas in which Singapore must learn from America. He finished by explaining that the problem in America is that poor children are not brought along and the very bright are allowed to coast.

The United States is currently caught up in a frenzy of test based reform, ostensibly aimed at those who most need not to be "left behind"—those who are not "brought along." The problem is that this authoritarian model, which emphasizes the achievement of the left brain, is doomed to failure—along with many of these same children. But it will *not* be the failure of students not testing well. There is every indication that when emphasis is placed upon tests, the scores increase. Just ask Singapore. But here's the big question: Will this increase lead to increased life success for these students?

That brings us back to the premise of Daniel Pink's work: that the future belongs to the creative. The "test and tremble" model of school reform that is the current craze, which values high scores over broader success, is unlikely to move us toward a more conceptual and creative society. In fact, with the emphasis placed so solidly on basic reading and math, the "right-brained" activities that Pink espouses (art, music, and creative expression) are being squeezed out of the curriculum.

The authoritarian model, which emphasizes the achievement of the left brain, is doomed to failure—along with many of these same children. But it will not *be the failure of students not testing well.*

Ellen Langer, in her book *Mindfulness,*[6] suggests that an education based on an outcomes model in fact leads to "mindlessness." She points out that from kindergarten on, the focus of schooling is usually on goals rather than on a process to achieve them. She points out that, "when children start a new activity with an outcome orientation, questions of 'can I' or 'what if I can't' are likely to predominate, creating an anxious preoccupation with success or failure rather than on drawing on the child's natural, exuberant desire to explore." Brain researchers tells us that fear inhibits cognitive ability by shutting down the synapses. A model of education based on coercive strategies is doomed to undo the very thing it is trying to accomplish: a smarter and more capable America.

The major goal of U.S. education under No Child Left Behind is to "close the achievement gap," a gap that is based on the same issues raised by the minister of education from Singapore—the fact that America has a large underclass that has not been educated to the highest possible levels. This problem is pretty universally accepted, both within our borders and beyond them. The question is whether an educational model that focuses on outcomes and deficits will close the gap or whether a different approach is called for—one that focuses on a broader definition of education and that focuses on assets.

The question is whether an educational model that focuses on outcomes and deficits will close the gap or whether a different approach is called for—one that focuses on a broader definition of education and that focuses on assets.

When it comes to poor and minority children, the irony of our current educational angst is that many of the same children who cannot read well can create and remember incredibly complex song lyrics set to hip hop music. In fact, much of America's creativity in music came from blues, jazz, rock and roll, and rap—all products of the so-called underclass. Moreover, children who cannot spell "systems thinking" may demonstrate an understanding of the movement of 10 people on the basketball court who are moving through time and space at high speeds, and may be able to anticipate future moves and create elegant responses to them on the run. This is the epitome of systems thinking. Children with limited English proficiency, who have trouble following a teacher's instructions, can shift language and culture numerous times a day. Native American children who have trouble with basic math can create intricate designs and artistic creations.

The good news is that much of America's creative expression has come from the very people we worry about not having a great left-brain education. This comes at a time when right-brain education and right-brain skills would appear to be in great demand. The assets that are already there simply need to be nourished and nurtured.

Is there not a way for America to rediscover its competitive edge—not by becoming more like the Asians, but by being more like Americans? Is there not a way to use the inherent talents that many of our underperforming children have in nonschool activities and bring those into the classroom, by helping teachers focus on the assets the children have and by honoring their thinking skills and way of looking at the world?

Wouldn't this provide us with the ultimate "out-of-the-box" experience?

NOTES

1. Friedman, T. L. (2006). *The world is flat: A brief history of the twenty-first century.* New York: Farrar, Straus and Giroux.

2. Pink, D. (2005). *A whole new mind: Moving from the Information Age to the Conceptual Age.* New York: Riverhead Books.

3. Florida, R. (2002). *The rise of the creative class.* New York: Basic Books.

4. Lemonick, M. D. (2006, February 13). Are we losing our edge? *Time, 167*(7), 22–33.

5. Zakaria, F. (2006, January 9). We all have a lot to learn. *Newsweek, 167*(2), 37.

6. Langer, E. (1989). *Mindfulness.* Cambridge, MA: Da Capo Press.

CHAPTER TWO

WHAT IT MEANS TO BE AN OUTSIDE-THE-BOX LEADER

DENNIS SPARKS

The difference between what we are doing and what we're capable of doing would solve most of the world's problems.

—Mahatma Gandhi

Probably the most important—and the most difficult—job of an instructional leader is to change the prevailing culture of a school.... A school's culture has far more influence on life and learning in the schoolhouse than the president of the country, the state department of education, the superintendent, the school board, or even the principal, teachers, and parents can ever have.

—Roland Barth

People take their emotional cues from the top.

—Daniel Goleman, Richard Boyatzis, and Annie McKee

B oxes are bounded spaces that by their very nature contain some things and exclude others. To the benefit of the organizations they lead, outside-the-box leaders see beyond the boundaries that both define and confine that space to reveal what may not have been previously evident. Such leaders see and address those boundaries that are visible (for example, structures, processes, and routines); they also name and therefore make visible those boundaries (mental models and other cultural forces) that were previously unrecognized.

One of a school leader's most important responsibilities is to see capacity that others overlook and to nurture its actualization. Human and organizational potential is often invisible. The human energy required to manifest potential may also lie dormant until it is activated by a compelling sense of purpose, stretching and compelling goals, an intense feeling of urgency for the accomplishment of those goals, and the human connections that create and sustain energy over time.

Outside-the-box leaders believe that their work matters. They know that what they think and how they consistently act makes a difference in the quality of teaching, learning, and relationships in their schools. They have faith in the power of their thoughts, words, and actions to truly make a difference in their schools. They understand that significant and lasting change in their organizations begins with significant and lasting change in what they think, say, and do.

Outside-the-box leaders know that what they think and how they consistently act makes a difference in the quality of teaching, learning, and relationships in their schools.

Consequently, these leaders regard their own development as a primary tool of organizational improvement and understand that who they are as human beings has a profound effect on the quality of their leadership. To that end, they deepen their understanding of important subjects and carefully cultivate habits of mind and behavior that further their purposes. They cultivate integrity in themselves and others and foster interpersonal accountability as a core cultural feature. For them, leadership is not simply a set of techniques, recipes, or scripts, but is instead a way of being in the world that by its very presence alters what occurs around it. Clarity, self-awareness, integrity, interpersonal accountability, passion, respect, and persistence are hallmarks of that presence. I will develop these ideas more fully below.

Outside-the-box leaders create clarity out of confusion, optimism and efficacy out of resignation, and interdependence out of dependence. A primary means by which leaders establish these conditions is through their influence on organizational culture, one of the most potent and least addressed influences on both thought and behavior within schools. To a large extent, school culture determines whether a school continuously improves itself or expends its energy in a futile effort to maintain the status quo. This chapter will explore leaders' influence on transforming organizational culture so that it opens itself to virtually limitless possibilities for staff performance and student learning.

ATTRIBUTES OF OUTSIDE-THE-BOX LEADERSHIP

Outside-the-box school leaders transform school cultures and structures that preserve the status quo to enable previously unrealized levels of accomplishment when they take the following actions:

1. Cultivate clarity regarding values and fundamental purposes.

2. Identify stretching and compelling goals.

3. Communicate fundamental choices, goals, and ideas.

4. View their work as a creative process.

5. Attend to the fundamental barriers that impede improvement.

6. Develop and display high levels of emotional and social intelligence.

7. Focus on the small things that make the biggest difference.

1. Cultivate clarity regarding the values and fundamental purposes that are most important to themselves and to their organizations. Outside-the-box leaders begin by developing greater clarity about their own "fundamental choices" based upon their deepest and most cherished purposes and values. Such clarity provides leaders and their organization with a sense of direction, power, and energy. They use their clarity as a filter through which they consider the desirability of collective beliefs, goals, and strategies.

Leaders' fundamental choices guide their actions. Such choices express their deepest aspirations.

Leaders' fundamental choices guide their actions. Such choices express their deepest aspirations, stimulate and sustain high performance, provide a filter for assessing the value of school improvement efforts, and sustain motivation during difficult times. "A fundamental choice," Robert Fritz (1989) writes in *The Path of Least Resistance,* "is a choice in which you commit yourself to a basic life orientation or a basic state of being" (p. 188). Fritz offers as examples being the predominant creative force in your life, being true to what is highest within you, and being healthy and free.

Primary choices, Fritz says, are those we make about the major results we wish to create, and secondary choices are the steps we take toward achieving those results. Primary choices are often called results, goals, or objectives. Secondary choices are strategies or action plans.

To make a similar point, Judith Wright (2005) uses the term "one decision" to describe a decision "about your life that will guide every single choice thereafter. This decision will impact the quality of your life, transforming the very fabric of your being" (p. 57). To illustrate, Wright suggests the following: "I live my life as if everything matters," "I connect with people and lead wherever I am," "I choose to care and to engage," and "I am truthful and genuine."

Outside-the-box leaders harness the power of fundamental choices or "one decisions" to motivate and sustain change. Robert Quinn (2000) describes the power of fundamental choices this way:

> The individuals, groups, teams, and organizations will not change until they can identify and embrace their potential, that is, really grasp what they are capable of achieving. This will not happen until one person, somewhere, makes a fundamental choice and begins to demonstrate a new way of being. This will result in new actions, words, and commitment. (p. 94)

This transformation occurs, Quinn contends, because our enthusiasm and commitment are contagious. He notes

> People around us are moved in ways that are subtle but powerful. We become living symbols of a new vision. We send out

new signals to everyone around us, and if we are in an organization, our very presence disrupts old routines. . . . A new dialogue is born and the culture in which we are participating
begins to change. (p. 113)

Here are a few examples of school leaders' fundamental choices
that are likely to produce such an effect:

- A superintendent makes a strong, public commitment that all
  students will have a competent, caring teacher—no exceptions, no excuses.
- A superintendent of a largely low-income and minority school
  system views teaching all students to read as literally a matter
  of life and death.
- A principal decides that the establishment of caring, supportive
  relationships among adults, among students, and between adults
  and students is of equal importance to the mastery of academics.
- A teacher leader serving as a mathematics coach in her school
  concludes that frequent candid conversations with colleagues
  about student learning and teaching methods will be at the
  center of her relationships with other teachers.

**2. Identify stretching and compelling goals for their own
work and for that of the organizations they lead.** Outside-the-box
leaders understand the value of goals that are sufficiently ambitious
to stretch their organization, compelling in ways that motivate staff
members to continuously improve their work, and are rich enough in
detail to guide planning and assessment of progress. The importance
of goal clarity is based on the complementary premises that people
move toward that which they are clearest about, and that it's very difficult to create that which we cannot describe in some detail.

Outside-the-box leaders understand that ambitious and compelling goals are necessary to produce the deep changes in beliefs
and practices that are important in improving the learning of all
students and in sustaining change over time. Stretch goals are important, they know, for the reason that most teachers and administrators
underestimate their ability to make improvements because it is
simply not possible for anyone to know all that is possible. That's
why goal-setting experts ask their clients to envision "wild success"
or to set goals for "paradise times four."

——————— ❦ ———————

Outside-the-box leaders understand that ambitious and compelling goals are necessary to produce the deep changes in beliefs and practices that are important in improving the learning of all students and in sustaining change over time.

High levels of achievement on the part of all students require deep changes in many parts of the organization, outside-the-box leaders know, and such changes require stretch goals. Successful attainment of stretch goals (some individuals use the term "BHAG" to prompt themselves to establish Big, Hairy, Audacious Goals), in turn, requires clarity of thought, unrelenting focus, consistent communication, alignment of resources, innovation, discipline, and teamwork.

For example, the goal that all students will read at grade level or higher when they leave a particular school—no matter their race or socioeconomic status—is likely to require significant alterations in curriculum, assessment, teaching methods, leadership practices, afterschool programs, and engagement with parents. Stretch goals are particularly powerful when they include incremental "milestones" that provide mid-course markers of improvement and offer opportunities to celebrate success and experience the motivation provided by that attainment.

As outside-the-box leaders know, goals that are richly detailed assist in planning (it is difficult to create that which you cannot describe) and in the assessment of progress. They describe what success will look like in the classroom or school. "There's power in detail," Dave Ellis (1998) reminds readers in *Creating Your Future: 5 Steps to the Life of Your Dreams.* "When your destination is clear, you're more likely to arrive there. When your goals are loaded with specifics, you're more likely to know when you've met them" (p. 27).

For instance, if the goal is the improvement of teaching and learning for all students, specificity enables backward mapping, from the desired student outcomes to the nature of teaching that will produce those outcomes to the type of professional learning that will enable all teachers to successfully use those approaches.

As an example, in *Teaching in the Knowledge Society,* Andy Hargreaves (2003) argues that it is essential that all students—black and white, rich and poor—acquire deep understanding, be creative and ingenious in their approaches to problem solving, be able to function in teams as well as independently, and learn to care about others so that they can make meaningful contributions to the public good as well as to their own welfare.

For schools to successfully nurture these qualities in students, Hargreaves says, "teachers must pursue deep and continuous professional learning, regularly exercise professional judgment, work in networks and teams, establish sustaining relationships with students and other teachers, draw on research, and make decisions based on shared data." The kind of professional development that produces such outcomes, Hargreaves believes, "requires time to understand, learn about, and reflect on what the change involves and requires. Even for the best teachers, changing successfully is hard intellectual work" (p. 108).

3. Communicate the fundamental choices, goals, and ideas that shape their work succinctly and powerfully through many media. While clarity of thought is essential, outside-the-box leaders understand the importance of their ability to express their thoughts in simple, declarative sentences for various purposes in a variety of settings.

In *The Cycles of Leadership: How Great Leaders Teach Their Companies to Win,* Noel Tichy (2002) uses the term "Teachable Points of Views" (TPOVs) to describe ideas expressed with clarity and precision, and the term "Interactive Teaching" to describe ways of interacting with others in the spirit of dialogue. The creation of TPOVs enables outside-the-box leaders to combine the solitary processes of introspection and reflection with community-based processes such as dialogue and consensus seeking to achieve organizationwide clarity about the values, ideas, and goals that are worthy of sustained effort and, when necessary, courageous action.

"[T]eaching is the most effective means through which a leader can lead," Tichy writes (p. 57). He adds, "[T]rue learning takes place only when the leader/teacher invests the time and emotional energy to engage those around him or her in a dialogue that produces mutual understanding" (p. 58). The starting point, Tichy says, is when "a leader commits to teaching, creates the conditions for being taught him or herself, and helps the students have the self confidence to engage and teach as well" (p. 21).

A TPOV, Tichy writes, is "a cohesive set of ideas and concepts that a person is able to articulate clearly to others" (p. 74). A TPOV reveals clarity of thought regarding ideas and values and is a tool for communicating them to others. Tichy believes it is critical that leaders have TPOVs on an "urgent need that is clear and palpable to everyone in the organization" (p. 85), "a mission that is inspiring and clearly worth achieving" (p. 86), "goals that stretch people's abilities" (p. 86), and "a spirit of teamwork" (p. 88). He also recommends that leaders develop TPOVs on the central ideas that will move the organization toward its goals, values that express the type of behavior desired by the organization, ways to generate positive emotional energy within the organization, and "edge" (the thought processes that inform tough yes/no decisions).

Tichy underscores the importance of clarity to leaders. "The very act of creating a Teachable Point of View makes people better leaders," he argues. "[L]eaders come to understand their underlying assumptions about themselves, their organization and business in general. When implicit knowledge becomes explicit, it can then be questioned, refined and honed, which benefits both the leaders and the organizations" (p. 97).

Outside-the-box leaders understand the importance of creating a clear, compelling point of view and are committed to the demanding intellectual work associated with its creation.

While outside-the-box leaders may not use the term "teachable point of view," they understand the importance of creating a clear, compelling point of view and are committed to the demanding intellectual work associated with its creation. They are also likely to appreciate the value of writing as a means of achieving clarity of thought and for communicating their points of view on important subjects. They may begin, for example, by committing to paper a few hundred words on key areas such as professional learning and collaboration in their schools, instructional leadership, quality teaching, the attributes of the relationships desired in the school among teachers and between teachers and students, and various means of assessing student progress in addition to standardized tests.

Or leaders may have taken the advice offered by outside-the-box leader Dennis Littky in *The Big Picture: Education is Everyone's Business* (2004):

> [S]tart right now by creating your own vision of how your school might become a great school. Start this as an internal dialogue, use the margins of this book or a journal to sketch out your first

ideas, and then get together with people around you and begin to build a collective vision. Imagine what your school would look like if the changes you imagine began to take hold. Live off that beauty and let it push you on. (p. 195)

Leaders develop TPOVs on important subjects that vary in length from five-minute "vision speeches" to day-long interactive teaching events to brief presentations for faculty meetings and parent get-togethers. A leader can also gather a school's leadership team and create common TPOVs around central ideas and values.

Stories with a plot line and cast of characters provide a powerful means by which TPOVs can be explained, illustrated, and understood in human terms. Tichy (2002) recommends the following:

At the same time that leaders are creating and constantly improving their TPOVs, they must also craft them into stories that are not only intellectually clear, but emotionally engaging, so that other people will be eager and willing to participate in the Virtuous Teaching Cycle that will make everyone smarter and faster and more aligned. (p. 131)

Tichy advocates three types of stories:

First, Who am I? (to explain the real-life experiences that have shaped the leader and his or her TPOVs)

Second, Who are we? (to describe the common experiences and beliefs of those in the organization)

Third, Where are we going? (to show what the organization is aiming to do and how it is going to do it)

4. View their work as a creative process as well as a technical task. Outside-the-box leaders act on the premise that educators' capacity to invent solutions to educational problems is a powerful, untapped resource for improvement. As a result, they view their schools as invention machines rather than simply as implementers of solutions imposed from the outside. They know that engagement in creative processes energizes and increases teachers' and administrators' commitment to continuous improvement.

———————— ⚜ ————————

Outside-the-box leaders view their schools as invention machines rather than simply as implementers of solutions imposed from the outside.

Outside-the-box leaders concur with Robert Fritz (1991), who observes the following in his book *Creating*: "The act of creating can bring out the best in people, because it is the natural motivator. No pep talk in the world, no matter how inspired, can touch the power of the involvement that creating generates" (p. 255). They also concur with Robert Quinn's views that "Our greatest joy no matter what our role comes from creating. In that process people become aware that they are able to do things they once thought were impossible. They have empowered themselves, which in turn empowers those with whom they interact" (quoted in Sparks, 2004, p. 51).

While valuing the creative capacity of teachers, outside-the-box leaders understand that schools also benefit from interacting with practitioners from other schools and with researchers or other sources of outside knowledge and skills. In fact, their experience has been that the more deeply they appreciate the talents that already reside in the school and initiate cultural changes that promote that appreciation and the sharing of effective practices, the more the school actively reaches out to other schools and to the professional literature as a source of energy and guidance.

Outside-the-box leaders understand that organizational creativity is diminished when schools select modest outcomes because the faculty does not believe that more ambitious goals can be achieved; when planners define current reality through opinions and anecdotes rather than rigorous analysis of various types of disaggregated data; and when schools select strategies for improvement without thorough, tough-minded discussions about their ability to produce the intended outcome. To counter such problems, these leaders cultivate teachers' professional knowledge and judgment by engaging them in sustained study of professional literature and in dialogue and debate regarding vision, stretch goals, current reality, and the selection of the most powerful strategies available to achieve those goals.

5. Attend to the fundamental barriers that impede continuous improvement. Because outside-the-box leaders understand the connections between seemingly disconnected things and constantly strive for a deeper and more nuanced understanding of important issues, they tend to look beneath the surface of things to detect and remedy the root causes of problems. Commonly cited barriers to sustained reform in schools are lack of money and time, state and federal mandates and regulations, recalcitrant teachers or teacher unions, and principals and district administrators who lack desire or skill in leading such efforts.

Outside-the-box leaders understand the connections between seemingly disconnected things. They tend to look beneath the surface of things to detect and remedy the root causes of problems.

Outside-the-box leaders understand that such large and seemingly intractable barriers often leave educators feeling helpless and hopeless, so they focus their efforts on more fundamental barriers: a lack of clarity regarding values, intentions, and beliefs; dependence on those outside of schools for solutions to problems; and a sense of resignation that robs educators of the energy that is essential to the continuous improvement of teaching, learning, and relationships in schools. Because these leaders also understand that these barriers lie within their circles of influence, they know that their beliefs, understanding, and actions can introduce clarity, interdependence among members of the school community, and a sense of possibility and optimism about the future.

Earlier in this chapter, I discussed the importance of leaders' clarity. The barrier of dependence means that teachers and principals wait for others to direct their actions, a form of "learned helplessness" that is a by-product of school reform initiatives based on mandates and compliance. While schools can benefit from synergistic relationships with district offices, universities, and other educational entities, for many schools the balance between internal and external sources of knowledge and action has become so distorted that those in schools no longer see themselves as initiators of action, generators of knowledge, or inventors of solutions to problems. Mike Schmoker (2004) laments the culture of dependency in schools; he observes that "I routinely encounter teachers and administrators who are waiting, endlessly, needlessly, for the right research or staff development programs" (p. 87).

Resignation is an intellectual and emotional state in which educators come to believe that their individual and collective actions cannot improve teaching and learning, particularly given the large and serious problems that affect the lives of many students and their families. "Low sense of efficacy" is a term that researchers use to describe this state. A profound consequence of this belief is that teachers and administrators act as if they have a very small, or perhaps even nonexistent, circle of influence related to student learning.

Outside-the-box leaders understand that lack of clarity as well as feelings of dependence and resignation are learned, which means that they can be replaced with new learning. Therefore, they

- expend effort to achieve clarity about organizational values, goals, and assumptions;
- create goals that are sufficiently large and compelling that their achievement requires interdependent action;
- counter resignation by enlarging their own sense of possibility and optimism through reading (for instance, reading biographies of individuals who overcame significant barriers in the pursuit of worthy goals) and study (particularly of research or other professional literature related to schools that have overcome significant barriers to improve student achievement); and
- participate in an ongoing community of supportive colleagues. I address these processes in much greater detail in *Leading for Results: Transforming Teaching, Learning, and Relationships in Schools* (Sparks, 2004).

6. Develop and display high levels of emotional and social intelligence and cultivate their inner lives as a reliable source of inspiration and guidance. Outside-the-box leaders develop their emotional and social intelligence so that they effectively manage the relationship demands of an intensively people-oriented job. In addition, they view effective leadership as a "way of being" in one's work that authorities in this area describe as authentic and "whole." Leadership, from this perspective, is as much or more about who leaders are as it is about what they do because school leaders' emotions and the quality of their relationships profoundly affect the organizations they lead.

Outside-the-box leaders understand that emotions are contagious. That means that leaders' positive energy—their enthusiasm and optimism, for instance—spreads to others. Likewise, their anger, anxiety, or sadness can infect others throughout the organization. These leaders know that awareness of their emotions and their ability to manage them in ways that serve their organizations' goals are a critically important and often overlooked aspect of their work.

The view that leadership is emotional and social as well as technical, and that it is profoundly influenced by qualities that are *inside* leaders, has important impli-

Outside-the-box leaders understand that emotions are contagious. That means that leaders' positive energy—their enthusiasm and optimism, for instance—spreads to others.

cations for the ways in which outside-the-box leaders develop themselves. In *Primal Leadership: Learning to Lead With Emotional Intelligence,* Daniel Goleman, Richard Boyatzis, and Annie McKee (2002) point out that leaders can develop their social and emotional skills by engaging in "five discoveries":

1. Uncovering an ideal vision of themselves

2. Discovering who they really are

3. Developing an agenda for improving their abilities

4. Practicing new leadership skills

5. Developing supportive and trusting relationships that make change possible

Outside-the-box leaders know that their identity, integrity, and inner wisdom are important sources of direction and influence in the school community. They understand that students and teachers want to know whether leaders are "real" and can be trusted. Students and teachers also size up leaders' genuineness by assessing, for instance, if leaders are truly compassionate rather than merely reciting a conversation formula that they were taught. Genuineness demonstrates caring.

Such an inside-out view of leadership recognizes the reciprocal influence between what is inside leaders and what occurs around them. In *A Hidden Wholeness,* Parker Palmer (2004) writes

If *you* are in the room, your *values* are in there too—if you do not believe that, you have not been paying attention. . . . What are we sending from within ourselves out into the world, and what impact is it having "out there"? What is the world sending back at us, and what impact is it having "in here"? . . . [W]e have the power to choose, moment by moment, between that which gives life and that which deals death. (p. 48)

Thomas Beech (quoted in Intrator, 2005) describes it this way: "Every person is grounded with an inner source of truth. . . . Our inner life of mind and spirit is interrelated with our outer life of action and service" (p. 87).

Outside-the-box leaders cultivate their inner lives by

- periodically reflecting on their values and strengths. They think seriously about the values that guide their lives and work and link them to important decisions. Likewise, they consciously think about and embrace the strengths they bring to their work and consider ways they might apply them more deliberately;
- listening deeply to themselves. These leaders create spaces in their lives in which they may receive the wisdom and understanding that can best be heard in solitude, silence, and reflective activities. Journal writing, quiet walks in nature, and meditation are just a few examples of such activities;
- listening to others. One of the greatest gifts these leaders give others in their organizations is committed listening during which they strive to absorb what others have to say without distraction, judgment, or a desire to fix or "save" the speaker. When they do so, they cultivate and deepen their appreciation of the human condition, a wellspring from which their wisdom grows;
- speaking their truths. Outside-the-box leaders know that their authenticity is a potent source of influence and that honesty is at the heart of authenticity. They also know that their inner wisdom is diminished when it is not shared. On this subject, Parker Palmer (2004) writes, "[W]e grant authority to people we perceive as 'authoring' their own words and actions, people who do not speak from a script or behave in preprogrammed ways" (pp. 76–77);
- living an examined life. Taken together, these suggestions describe "the examined life." The dialogue between the inner and outer aspects of these leaders' lives is a source of profound professional learning and guidance that enriches their work and the work of the schools they lead.

7. Focus relentlessly on a small number of things that make the largest difference. Outside-the-box leaders have learned to attend to the few things that are most influential in achieving their most important goals. They have learned, as Stephen Covey (2004) puts it, "to distinguish between what is 'merely important' and what is 'wildly important'" (p. 281).

Outside the box leaders have developed the ability to discriminate between the things that make an important contribution to the achievement of the organization's goals and everything else—and the capacity to focus on the former category. A term given to this way of thinking is "the 80/20 principle" (also known as "the Pareto principle").

"The 80/20 Principle asserts that a minority of causes, inputs, or effort usually lead to a majority of the results, outputs, or rewards," Richard Koch (1998) claims in *The 80/20 Principle: The Secret to Success by Achieving More With Less* (p. 4). He adds, "Unless you use the 80/20 Principle to redirect your strategy, you can be pretty sure that the strategy is badly flawed" (pp. 24–25). Koch argues that

——————— ✒ ———————

Outside-the-box leaders have developed the ability to discriminate between the things that make an important contribution to the achievement of the organization's goals and everything else—and the capacity to focus on the former category.

> 80 percent of achievement is attained in 20 percent of the time taken. . . . 80 percent of happiness is experienced in 20 percent of life. . . . Remember that these are hypotheses to be tested against your experience. . . . It doesn't matter [what] the exact percentages are and in any case it is almost impossible to measure them precisely. The key question is whether there is a major imbalance between the time spent on the one hand and achievement or happiness on the other. (pp. 146–147)

Outside-the-box leaders are well above average in their ability to eliminate or minimize the "80 percent activities" that produce modest results and to devote their energy to high-value activities. They understand, as Koch puts it, that "it is often tiny amounts of time that make all the difference" (p. 149).

Mike Schmoker (2005) describes how Rick DuFour, then a high school principal, altered his leadership from time-consuming, low-impact tasks, such as classroom observations with pre-observation and postobservation meetings, to a small number of activities focused on student learning. According to Schmoker, DuFour required teachers to identify and focus on a limited number of essential concepts and topics, provided teachers with both in-school data and evidence of how other comparable schools were performing, asked teachers to use data to focus on targeted areas for improvement, arranged for teachers to meet twice a month to prepare and improve lessons based on the results of formative assessments, met with teams on a regular basis to inquire about student learning, and rewarded and celebrated progress at faculty meetings.

At the core of such an approach, Schmoker contends, is leadership that ensures a guaranteed and viable curriculum for all students, establishes self-managing teams, and expects teaching to be adjusted based on regular formative assessments.

WAYS SCHOOL SYSTEMS CAN CULTIVATE OUTSIDE-THE-BOX LEADERSHIP

The development of district and school leaders—both administrators and teacher leaders—is one of a school system's most important responsibilities. Such efforts cannot guarantee that all leaders will perform "outside the box," however. (And because out-of-the-box leaders often push the boundaries of accepted thought and practice, I'm not certain that very many school systems would want too many such individuals.) But, when combined with clear standards and systems of accountability, such leaders can ensure continuous improvements in leadership practice.

Unfortunately, many school systems operate from the view that good leaders are born, not made. In these districts, leadership development is a neglected stepchild compared to teacher development, which more often than not suffers from its own serious problems. Leaders in such systems often lack a deep understanding of the attributes of high-quality teacher development because their own professional learning is woefully inadequate.

> *Unfortunately, many school systems operate from the view that good leaders are born, not made. In these districts, leadership development is a neglected stepchild.*

School systems with cutting-edge leadership development efforts typically combine several of the following elements:

- A systemwide culture of community, candor, integrity, experimentation, and continuous improvement. Such a culture is established and maintained by the superintendent and other senior district leaders

- Leaders' learning, embedded in the act of instructional leadership and culture building in their schools. Leaders don't just "learn about" instructional leadership or community building by passively sitting at the feet of experts, although experts or external organizations may be used periodically to introduce essential knowledge or skills to leaders. Instead, leaders learn by doing when they engage, as part of their daily work, in continuous cycles of action and reflection. Through such efforts, school leaders learn how to use relevant data in planning and decision making, how to talk with teachers about student work, and how to work with teachers in creating formative classroom assessments of student learning that lead to improved teaching, among other skills.

- Team-focused learning for leaders. Leaders meet regularly with other administrators in their districts to learn, practice new skills, and solve ongoing problems of improving instruction and shaping school culture. Teams typically meet in participants' schools and focus their skill-building and discussion on core processes of instructional leadership such as classroom "walk-throughs" or the use of protocols to assess student work. They may also be part of ongoing regional, state, or national teams to expand the sources of their learning and to broaden their professional network.

- Persistence in achieving greater clarity of thought about important ideas and values that are central to the continuous improvement of teaching and learning. Leaders develop and articulate orally and in writing their views regarding the types of student learning sought in their schools, the type of teaching that produces that learning, and their role as instructional leaders in the school. Related to those topics, they also learn how to engage others in cycles of dialogue-based learning that produce new ways of thinking and acting in the organization.

- Individualized assistance in the form of mentoring and coaching to assist leaders with the day-to-day challenges of their work. Such one-to-one forms of support are often essential to leaders' success and retention in their jobs, particularly for administrators who are new to their roles.

* Attention to the interpersonal and emotional aspects of leadership. Because leaders' relationship skills and emotional qualities have a profound effect on the communities they lead, administrators develop self-awareness in these areas and create plans to acquire or strengthen interpersonal and communication skills.

Taken together, these approaches acknowledge that leaders' sustained learning is essential in improving teaching and learning in all classrooms by immersing leaders in substantive and sustained conversations about their work. High-quality leadership development cultivates the essential attributes of outside-the-box leadership—clarity of purpose, a sense of possibility and efficacy, and the interdependence that generates energy and interpersonal accountability. Without skillful leadership that is developed through such efforts, high levels of learning for all students will remain an aspiration rather than a reality for the youngsters who are now in our schools.

REFERENCES

Covey, S. (2004). *The 8th habit: From effectiveness to greatness.* New York: Free Press.

Ellis, D. (1998). *Creating your future: 5 steps to the life of your dreams.* New York: Houghton Mifflin.

Fritz, R. (1989). *The path of least resistance.* New York: Fawcett Columbine.

Fritz, R. (1991). *Creating.* New York: Fawcett Columbine.

Goleman, D., Boyatzis, R., & McKee, A. (2002). *Primal leadership: Learning to lead with emotional intelligence.* Boston: Harvard Business School Press.

Hargreaves, A. (2003). *Teaching in the knowledge society: Education in the age of insecurity.* New York: Teachers College Press.

Intrator, S. (Ed.). (2005). *Living the questions: Essays inspired by the work and life of Parker J. Palmer.* San Francisco: Jossey-Bass.

Koch, R. (1998). *The 80/20 principle: The secret to success by achieving more with less.* New York: Doubleday.

Littky, D. (2004). *The big picture: Education is everyone's business.* Alexandria, VA: Association for Supervision and Curriculum Development.

Palmer, P. (2004). *A hidden wholeness: The journey toward an undivided life.* San Francisco: Wiley.

Quinn, R. (2000). *Change the world: How ordinary people can accomplish extraordinary results.* San Francisco: Jossey-Bass.

Schmoker, M. (2004). *Learning communities at the crossroads: Toward the best schools we've ever had. Phi Delta Kappan, 86*(1), 84–88.

Schmoker, M. (2005). *The new fundamentals of leadership. SEDL Letter, 17*(2), 3–7.

Sparks, D. (2004). *Leading for results: Transforming teaching, learning, and relationships in schools.* Thousand Oaks, CA: Corwin Press.

Tichy, N. (2002). *The cycles of leadership: How great leaders teach their companies to win.* New York: Harper Business.

Wright, J. (2005). *The one decision: Make the single choice that will lead to a life of more.* New York: Penguin.

CHAPTER THREE

CARING, SERVING . . . LEADING

LES M. OMOTANI

To lead out of the box, one must learn how to *think* outside of the box. What we think about the world, our relationships, and our work directly influences our behaviors and how others interact with us as leaders. If we possess the ability to see the system below the surface or in multiple dimensions, if we are able to envision a desirable future, then we'll be able to lead "outside of the box."

THE POWER OF BELIEVING

Some of the most honest and useful feedback I have received has come from those very special teachers and staff members who have taken the risk to be both a colleague and a friend. These wonderful educators have shared the same advice: "Keep speaking from the heart!"

Think about the common wisdom that superintendents should not be friends with teachers and staff. Think about what this line of wisdom is intended to accomplish and prevent. If you are able to think outside of the box, this so-called wisdom is merely a silly limitation. If I truly care about people, and spend over 80 hours a week with some of them, developing honest relationships and sharing common aspirations and goals, why wouldn't some of them become my friends?

"But you might favor your friends!" becomes the refrain. If you think abundance rather than scarcity, there will always be more than enough support to be given to all. And if your ethical and moral base is strong and right, you will never allow friendship to take priority over doing what is right for the students who are in your care.

We aspire to the role of superintendent in order to make a positive difference for students. I learned my most important lesson in life and leadership from my first-grade teacher, Leona Kemper-Christiansen. She believed in the promise and mission of public education. She looked past my obvious "signs" of race and poverty. Mrs. Kemper decided on my first day of school that I would learn to sing and read—a lot.

Being in Mrs. Kemper's first-grade class provided a very important lesson in out-of-the-box leadership. She was indeed a leader, not a follower or a manager. She saw potential when others saw a challenging student. She thought opportunity when others were thinking, "what a challenge!" She believed in her ability to make a positive difference when others were looking for someone or something to blame.

I learned that everything I am, have, and get to do as an adult is because great teachers and leaders like Mrs. Kemper believed in the mission and promise of public education: that every child can and will learn, achieve, and perform.

Shigato Na

While Mrs. Kemper's leadership lesson was fundamental, an even earlier out-of-the-box lesson in leadership was taught to me by my grandfather. I'm not even sure if the phrase he used—"shigato na"—was real or one he made up for the occasion. I just know it was his standard answer when I asked him why he wasn't upset or angry about the past. I kept asking the question in different ways, and he always had the same answer: "shigato na."

My grandfather was a Canadian citizen who was interned during World War II after being declared an enemy alien. Nothing could have been further from the truth. But this was wartime, and people were scared. My grandfather was a very successful farmer and businessman. At one time he owned a large part of the land that today is Vancouver International Airport. During these years, he hired and supervised over 300 workers. He also owned a commercial fishing boat and his own home.

When World War II began, his life was changed forever. Almost everything he had owned was taken from him. In an instant, he lost his sense of citizenship, ownership, and security. His daughter—my newly married mother—lost her new home, all of her wedding presents, new English furniture and china, and new appliances and clothes.

And yet my grandfather remained a leader. He *thought* differently from most of those around him. He reminded everyone in the family of a few simple truths that had not changed:

- America is a great country.
- The promise of public education is that every child can learn, achieve, and perform, regardless of his or her family background or socioeconomic class.
- Family is more important than possessions.
- "Shigato na," which he explained to me with the following words: "You cannot go back and change the past. What is done is done! You can only choose how you wish to see and think about your future. *What you think about is what you will do and become in the future.* If you imagine everything as being possible, you will help others to have a good life."

My grandfather made a decision to keep his family together, took a train from British Columbia to Alberta, put on his best tuxedo, top hat, and white gloves, and prepared to meet a Czechoslovakian-Canadian immigrant family who would give him a new start, a new opportunity, to build a new farm and a new life. My grandfather treated this farmer, who was dressed in mud-covered boots, blue jeans, a denim shirt, and a straw hat, as if he were a prime minister or the president. He did not waste one word complaining of the injustices or events that had led him to this land of hot summers and bitterly cold winters. Instead, he expressed gratitude, loyalty, dedication, hope, and optimism. He dedicated himself to being a great worker and farmer. He readily made the transition from owner to worker. My grandfather was grateful to the thinking of this farmer who operated out of an abundance mentality rather than thoughts of scarcity.

Imagine the thinking that was necessary, on the part of a new immigrant farmer, to embrace a stranger in need and to offer to share his precious land. My grandfather understood this kind of thinking, and he repeated to his family the creed of "shigato na."

> *Out-of-the-box leaders have the choice and the ability to focus on the future and not dwell on the past. . . . What matters most is what a leader will do today and tomorrow to improve the educational experience for each of our students.*

My grandfather's thinking applies to the task of leading educational improvement efforts today. Out-of-the-box leaders have the choice and the ability to focus on the future and not dwell on the past. It really doesn't matter why the system is the way it is today. What matters most is what a leader will do today and tomorrow to improve the educational experience for each of our students.

Prior to this lesson from my grandfather, it was my father who taught me another early lesson of leadership. He too believed that the way in which you think determines how you see the world—and thus how you will behave, serve, and lead.

My father taught me the concept of "face," or honor. Honor to him was not about achieving ribbons, medals, trophies, or prizes. Honor was about how a person thinks about the concepts of honesty, integrity, and loyalty. My father taught me that all work is honorable, whether that work is with the hands or the mind. He taught me to think about the task of digging a latrine (the Western outhouse) as honest work, to be done with quality and gratitude. He taught me to value and to appreciate everyone's contribution and never to believe that a task—any task—was not worth my time or effort.

LEADERSHIP

Leadership is a function that creates the support and conditions that allow people within an organization or community to learn and achieve their goals. Leadership is different from management. Leaders must be effective managers. However, being an effective manager is not sufficient to be a leader.

Leaders think about and see both systems and the future in different ways than managers.

I believe that whatever dominates our thinking will dominate our leadership style, our values, and our actions. When we simply react to issues, we tend to see everything as a management problem to be solved. When we focus on a shared vision, and the desired culture for our schools and community, we open the door for leadership.

It may be an oversimplification, but if you want out-of-the-box leadership, you must generate and encourage out-of-the-box thinking!

When everyone around you is thinking about test scores and accountability, out-of-the-box leaders are reflecting on such things as integrated learning experiences, authentic assessment, performance portfolios, music and the arts, higher-order thinking, and organizational cultural values such as caring.

Here's an example: At the end of a very long day, after a very positive evening meeting of the Board of Education, I was leaving my office, had descended the stairs, and was about to exit through the security door of the building. I was thinking about how early I would have to get up the next morning to catch a scheduled flight, and how precious would be the few hours available for sleep. Just before I opened the door, I thought, in an instant, about the people and the things we had celebrated that evening and the importance of caring relationships. Immediately, I ran back up the steps and into the meeting room to thank the custodian who was engaged in her normal routine of cleaning up after all of us and straightening out the room. It took only a few moments to ask how she was doing, to help throw away some trash on the tables, and to put a few chairs into a stack. My few words of appreciation were greeted with the response, "It's my job! Thank you!" and a smile big enough to fill a room.

It's my job! Thank you! Smile! Those are the rewards for taking the time to think about caring relationships. If I had not thought about the value of caring, I would have jumped into my vehicle and sped down the road, dwelling on the few hours of sleep left in the night. Instead, I floated down the stairs and outside, thankful that a simple instantaneous thought had compelled me back up the stairs and into a room occupied by one of the most important, dedicated, and positive employees in our organization.

————————— ❦ —————————

I think about caring *as a core organizational value.*

I think about *caring* as a core organizational value. Doing so allows me to think about the possibility and the desirability of leading the development of one of the most caring communities of learners in the nation. I think about what is required to engage members of a system in a conversation about a way of doing things, about the kind of organization and culture that lead to a high level and quality of caring relationships. I think about what is required to decide to commit the time and effort necessary to lead a shared visioning process that asks members to share their aspirations, hopes, and dreams of the kind of system, organization, or community in which they wish to learn and work every day, week, month, and year.

That, to me, is out-of-the-box leadership.

OUT-OF-THE-BOX LEADING

The following examples serve to illustrate the kinds of thinking that are associated with out-of-the-box leadership:

• Time is the enemy of good intentions. How do you create time for out-of-the-box thinking? Out-of-the-box leaders work within the same 24-hour day as every other superintendent. They just seem to have more time because they tend to smile more of the time than their management-oriented colleagues. The simple act of allocating time for visioning, planning, and reflection is an out-of-the-box leadership habit. Out-of-the-box leaders actually schedule time for planning and thinking.

• Paperwork will always be on your desk waiting for you. Students, teachers, and staff are only available during the daytime, when school is in session. Out-of-the-box leaders are often heard proclaiming the importance of all students and all employees. These leaders spend time with employees. As Walt Whitman said, "We convince with our presence." Though it can be difficult to walk the talk, if you say, "Our kids and people are important," then you must schedule the time to be among and with them.

BEING PRESENT

If you think your main job is to deal with the paperwork on your desk and answer the hundreds of emails that clutter your computer screen each day, then you will spend all of your time in your chair behind your desk. If you think that your leadership role is to pay attention to students, teachers, administrators, staff, and the community, then you will spend your time visiting classrooms, attending school activities, talking with and listening to teams of staff and administrators, and participating in community functions. I think that walking the talk in small but significant steps is more important than writing and saying big manifestos. In fact, I have found that the more time I spend trying to "walk the talk," the less time I spend talking and writing! When you spend your time observing and listening to others, you really don't need to say very much at all!

Leadership is an avocation and a vocation. I love what I get to do! I get to care for and serve others all my days! Think about the difference between an organization and leadership that pays attention to everyone rather than one that only caters to a few. Think about the impact of saying to a neglected group of employees, "I know you are really busy at this time of the year, but you are every bit as important as the teachers and the administrators in this district. We are meeting to welcome them back to the beginning of the new year, and it is important to us that we also meet with you. Again, I know you are busy with lots of items on your to-do lists, but I will not apologize for bringing you together and sharing with you the same information that we have shared with the rest of our team and family." Think about the impact of telling these valued and often overlooked employees that they work for an organization that supports their desire to come together, share some food, and sit in a comfortable setting to meet their colleagues and discuss the opportunities of the new year. Think about the fact that your employees really do want to come together and build caring relationships. Think about it!

The feedback to these kinds of actions is immediate and overwhelmingly positive. Strong handshakes, the gleam in their eyes, the

> Leadership is an avocation and a vocation. *I love what I get to do! I get to care for and serve others all my days!*

positive tone of voice that says, "We're ready to go, Doc," and the sincerest "Thank you for taking the time—we know you are busy!" Think about why you chose to serve and lead. Think about how much you care.

VISITING CLASSROOMS

Everyone visits classrooms. But what do you think about when you are visiting those classrooms? Out-of-the-box leaders look for things to praise rather than things to criticize. They ask of themselves, "What can I or our organization do to help these people be more effective and successful?" They take the time to interact with the children and build relationships. Out-of-the-box leaders listen to the children's stories. They sit on the floor and ask a lot of questions. They take detailed notes about what they were thinking so that they can give positive feedback to the teacher later that day.

I became a teacher because I wanted to make a positive differ- ence in the lives of children. I became an administrator because I wanted to support others who wanted to make a positive difference in the lives of children. I used to think that an administrator worked outside the classroom. I now think that some of my most important and successful work is accomplished by visiting classrooms and interacting with our students.

I will share a secret about visiting classrooms: It's a lot of fun and very rewarding. Many times it yields the best feelings and expe- riences I have in a day or week. It's a secret because many leaders who visit classrooms rarely tell others how much they enjoy it. This is because most people think work is supposed to be tough, boring, challenging, and frustrating.

SERVANT LEADERSHIP

Fifteen years ago, I wrote a mission statement for my life and pro- fessional goals that was several pages in length. Today I live by five simple words: *He cared and he served!*

Think about the power and the pleasure of waking up every day and anticipating the opportunities that await to care for and serve others. Caring is not dependent on the availability of resources.

Service places the leader in a support position that ultimately provides great influence. Think about what it takes to create a culture of commitment rather than compliance—a culture in which people do things because they truly *want* to do them, not because they are fearful or feel they *have* to do them.

SYSTEMS THINKING

Peter Senge changed my life with a simple set of phrases and concepts. First, he said, "It's not what the vision is but what the vision does that matters most of all!" (personal communication, July 1996). In other words, it doesn't matter what the words in a vision statement are. Words on a sheet of paper that everyone agrees to are not a shared vision. It's just a piece of paper. What is much more important is the powerful mental image, the energy, and the excitement surrounding what is to become that evolves when people at every level of the organization are engaged in an ongoing process of talking about what really matters to them.

And second, Senge's fifth discipline, or core competence for learning organizations, is systems *thinking.* Developing the capacity and the constant desire to *think* about the system and to practice systems thinking are core leadership competencies. If we understand that the laws of ecology are non-negotiable and that systems constantly are in search of balance, then our perceptions of our roles as leaders begin to change. We begin to understand that our leadership responsibility is for the entire community, and that we must be concerned with the future of our children's children's children.

SUSTAINABILITY

The leaders who built cathedrals and castles knew that they would never live long enough to worship or live in the structures they began to build. Their thinking was long term; they thought about their children's children's children's future.

If we think about what is necessary and desirable to create a high-quality sustainable future for our children's children's children, we will make different choices and decisions than if we think only about the short term. We will serve and lead in a different manner. Think about this concept. It has the power to change your life!

Out-of-the-box leaders who think about sustainability take the time and make the effort to join students and teachers who are engaged in overnight field experiences learning about the environment, about natural systems and stewardship. Such programs are supported and valued as an integral component of the core curriculum. Out-of-the-box leaders put on their jeans and hiking boots and join sixth-grade students as they climb mountains, build shelters in the forest, and wade through streams. They help build the fire that is used to cook the hot dogs and hamburgers. They know how to make s'mores.

OUT OF THE BOX

When you first read "out of the box," did you envision a flat square on a piece of paper, or did you see a three-dimensional box? Was it in black and white or in color? Was it sitting on a table or floating in the air and spinning? How you think about a concept such as "out of the box" will determine how you lead.

Out-of-the-box leaders work at seeing problems as opportunities. They approach antagonists as partners. They invite challenging people to meet with them and engage in a thoughtful conversation (despite their initial desire to push back and ignore these individuals).

Out-of-the-box leaders work at seeing problems as opportunities. They approach antagonists as partners.

Thomas Crum, a Colorado Aikido master, views the power of engaging those with whom one disagrees as a dance. Rather than pushing adversaries away, bring them closer. Even though your first inclination may be to argue or to be defensive, an Aikido philosophy causes you to think in terms of wanting to truly understand the point of view of others. For example, if someone is yelling at you on the phone, ask if the person would mind your coming by his or her house to continue the conversation in person, thus enabling you to give the person the time and attention that he or she deserves. This kind of attempt to draw another closer in a dance of thoughtful conversation is an out-of-the-box leadership strategy that can have dramatic positive effects.

It's All About the Kids

Out-of-the-box leaders may admit that there was a period during their career when choices and decisions were sometimes made on the basis of ego-oriented goals. Transforming and letting go of the question, "But what about me?" is a significant milestone. I got out of the box when it was no longer about me. My service and leadership truly became focused solely on doing the right things right for the students and our community. Interestingly, I learned that a change in thinking led to an increase in courage, humility, and patience. As with many other changes in behavior, the result was a great amount of satisfaction and happiness experienced on a regular basis.

The Ladder of Inference

Out-of-the-box leaders practice and help others learn how to know when they are running up the "ladder of inference." Here's a simple example: You see your neighbor come home at noon, and soon after, a strange car pulls into the driveway and a very attractive woman enters the house. You know that your neighbor's wife is away because you saw her getting into a taxi with a suitcase, evidently headed for the airport, earlier this morning. The stranger's car remains in the driveway for two days.

What are your thoughts about this situation? Do you suspect the husband of being unfaithful? Are you ready to tell his wife upon her return? Do you share the information with others in the neighborhood?

Three days later, your neighbor's wife returns. You learn that she had to fly to another state to help care for her father who had had a serious accident. She expressed gratitude that her younger sister, a nurse, was available and willing to stay at her house and help her husband look after the children. One of the children had the chicken pox, so all of the kids had stayed home for a few days.

A diagram of the ladder of inference can be seen in Peter Senge's book *The Fifth Discipline Fieldbook* (1994). The rungs of the ladder (from bottom to top) include the following seven steps:

1. I capture observable data, unfiltered.

2. I select certain data from the scope of what I observe.

3. I add meaning.

4. I make assumptions.

5. I draw conclusions.

6. I adopt beliefs.

7. [top rung of the ladder] I take actions based on my beliefs.

By learning and practicing skills associated with the ladder of inference, out-of-the-box leaders and their staffs self-monitor and limit their own tendencies to "jump to conclusions." With practice and time, they develop the ability to skillfully "walk back down" the ladder and explore erroneous data, conclusions, assumptions, and beliefs.

ICEBERGS

Have you ever heard or used the phrase, "We don't have time to study this"? How many times do you encounter problems and issues that cause you to think, "We've been here before"? If you think you have a complete picture of complex problems as a result of a quick analysis or briefing, you are probably piloting your own version of the *Titanic*.

Being willing and able to see the whole system, to see below the surface of the water, is an out-of-the-box leadership skill. Conversations about deep systemic challenges, issues, and opportunities require careful planning, facilitation, and time for participants to gather information, analyze data, and engage in thoughtful dialogue.

The tip is the smallest part of the iceberg. It is what we see—events, problems, certain behaviors, situations. A more complete examination of the iceberg enables us to look below the surface and examine patterns and trends, systemic structures, and mental models that may be at the root of issues or problems people and organizations are experiencing. The iceberg is an excellent tool for groups to use in proactive problem solving.

BE GENUINE

One of the most difficult leadership actions is to resist being what and whom you *think* everyone wants you to be. Out-of-the-box leaders learn to be genuine and give themselves permission to be themselves. Small children and young adults know when leaders are being fake and when they are being real. They trust and support leaders who are being real.

The same thinking applies to relationships with staff, parents, and members of the community. The paradox is that, when we drop the veil of expected role and image behaviors, we gain increased trust and respect from all stake-holders.

When students want to spend time in the company of the super-intendent, it's a good indicator that the leader is being genuine. When

Out-of-the-box leaders learn to be genuine and give themselves permission to be themselves.

students go out of their way to say hello and to call the superinten-dent by name, it's an indicator that genuine relationships have been formed. When students are not being afraid of being seen interacting with the superintendent, it's a positive indicator that caring relation-ships have been developed.

BE GRATEFUL

Everything I am and get to do is because others believed in me and gave of themselves to help me learn and grow. They served as men-tors and models of what outstanding servant leaders do in their daily lives. I am grateful for the writings, thinking, teachings, and support of Robert Greenleaf, Peter Senge, Thomas Crum, Stephen Covey, W. Edwards Deming, William Ophuls, Nelda Cambron McCabe, and Beth Jandernoa. I am grateful for the teachers, staff, administra-tors, parents, and board members who have supported my develop-ment as a leader. I am grateful for the thousands of students who have given my life a calling and great purpose.

HABITS

One of the most important leadership decisions and acts that an out-of-the-box leader can make is to allocate time for others to engage in learning new skills and habits. If a system is to function out of a sense of common aspiration and vision rather than as a result of compliance measures, its people must be supported in their individual and team learning. This learning must be seen as a part of their regular work.

Developing new habits requires the opportunity to practice in a safe and supportive environment. The challenge is to continue to use the new behaviors during times of high stress, anxiety, and risk. You will know that you have "arrived" when you cannot remember thinking or being any other way!

CARING

Schools are places where caring relationships are essential to the effective nurturing and education of children. Perhaps more important, I believe that almost all people who belong to school systems and communities of learners *want* and need to have caring relationships in their lives.

By asking and answering a few simple questions, a community can begin to create its desired future. These questions help to structure a thoughtful dialogue:

What do we want to create?

What do we want to see happen here?

What needs to go away?

What do we want to keep and enhance?

What matters most of all?

Leaders who think out of the box will lead out of the box. Getting out of the box is necessary if we are to educate children to be successful in a world that is changing at an exponential rate. Today, more than in any previous years, leaders who dare to step outside of the box are finding themselves in the company of dedicated, competent, and visionary leaders who care for children and their communities.

YOUTH LEADERSHIP FORUM

Thinking out of the box provides the opportunity to create new learning experiences for high school students. Traditional thinking tends to focus on narrowing the curriculum and improving student test score results on state and federally mandated examinations. Thinking and believing that today's graduates need skills and experiences associated with systems thinking and servant leadership allow for the creation and implementation of programs such as the Youth Leadership Forum (YLF).

The allocation of time on out-of-the-box activities is critical for out-of-the-box leaders. In the Hewlett-Woodmere Public Schools, I cofacilitated, along with the high school principal, four six-day learning and practice sessions of 100 students and 10 adults. The YLF uses small-group and team processes and strategies to help the participants learn, practice, and develop desirable habits. The allocation of significant amounts of time by the superintendent, spent directly interacting with and supporting the learning of students, communicates leaders' belief in the importance of students.

Traditional thinkers (not out-of-the-box thinkers) might have limited the group size to a manageable 30 or 40—selecting only the brightest and the most involved students. But we decided to trust *all* of the students who wanted to become a part of the group. This meant that our numbers rose to over 100, but the group now reflects the wonderful diversity of the school. Student journals validate the meaningfulness and value of students' learning experiences. Over time, students themselves will become involved in cofacilitation of the group.

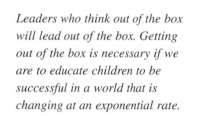

Leaders who think out of the box will lead out of the box. Getting out of the box is necessary if we are to educate children to be successful in a world that is changing at an exponential rate.

Out-of-the-box leaders use fables, simulations, and teambuilders from the world of systems thinking and learning organization. Students are actively engaged as participants in world café conversations, creating models of systems and using gallery walks to have a shared learning experience, and participating in physical collaborative challenges that are fun experiences but are also intended to develop their relationships within the community and their teams. Students are organized into small café groups of four participants. Large-group dialogue or "harvesting" occurs throughout each session in order to allow everyone to hear the thinking of the various teams.

GALLERY ONE AND WINTER CONCERTS

The arts and music are our most universal and essential forms of communication and expressive language. At a time when music and arts programs are being questioned, reduced, or eliminated throughout our nation, out-of-the-box leaders declare the arts to be a vital part of the core curriculum. Out-of-the-box leaders act in ways that demonstrate to all members of the learning community that the arts are valued and important.

Recently, the walls of the Woodmere Education Center (the administrative offices for the Hewlett-Woodmere Public Schools) became display spaces for student-created works of art. We offered and sponsored the creation of "Gallery One," comprising quick-change Plexiglas frames capable of displaying over 250 pieces of student art. Out-of-the-box leaders are not afraid to replicate great ideas that proved successful in other districts.

Several hundred students, parents, grandparents, and members of the community eagerly attended the opening evening of Gallery One. Visitors to the Woodmere Education Center readily saw that the arts are alive and valued in the Hewlett-Woodmere Public Schools. Each year, thousands of students receive a gallery display program and a VIP Artist Ribbon. In addition to the *a*rts, out-of-the-box leaders support the celebration of learning, achievement, and performance in the other three A's: *a*cademics, *a*thletics, and *a*ctivities.

Out-of-the-box leaders understand the impact of and difference between 80% attendance and perfect (100%) attendance during events such as the Winter Concert Series and the All-County Music Festival. One-hundred percent attendance means attending *all* of the concerts— each school, each grade level, each performance. Maintaining perfect attendance during arguably the busiest time of the year results in the unquestioned understanding by students, faculty, parents, and community that music education is important and valued. It is well understood by students, parents, staff, and the community that music education has in the leader a significant patron and sponsor.

CHILD-CENTERED PERSONALIZED LEARNING

Those in the teaching profession understand how children learn and develop. Their knowledge of how to appropriately and effectively personalize learning for each child is arguably at a high watermark in the history of our nation's schools. Out-of-the-box leaders continually bring the agenda and conversations back to these concepts. The tyranny of single test scores is attacked and diminished in systems led by out-of-the-box leaders.

Out-of-the-box leaders ensure that the teachers' and the district's own assessments matter most of all! These leaders ensure that communication plans and strategies are targeted to inform the community that the priority goals are associated with providing and developing breadth and depth in the four A's.

STUDENT OPPORTUNITY FUND

Even high-wealth suburban districts have hundreds or thousands of students who qualify for Title I support. Arguably the disparity in such districts can be as challenging as in systems where a majority of students qualify for Title I assistance.

Out-of-the-box leaders create special funds, supported by private donations. The funds are used to severely diminish and hopefully eliminate barriers that prevent some students from sharing special experiences enjoyed by most students. Out-of-the-box leaders create vehicles for philanthropic giving, such as the Student Opportunity Fund, so that students in need of financial assistance can easily and readily be supported.

When it comes time for gift giving (birthdays, special achievements, etc.), this fund provides individuals throughout the district the chance to benefit students by giving a gift in the name of an individual. Donor thank-you cards and notes to the individual being honored allow the Student Opportunity Fund to be thought of as a valued means of recognizing special people and occasions.

Out-of-the-box leaders support the enhancement of educational foundations and endowments. Out-of-the-box leaders model philanthropic habits and practices.

Out-of-the-box leaders ensure that the teachers' and the district's own assessments matter most of all!

THEY ARE MY KIDS

The world of work and life in the twenty-first century does not allow some parents to be present for some very special events and times in their children's school experiences. Out-of-the-box leaders take the time and effort to ensure that each child has a caring adult present to applaud, cheer, listen, and encourage during these special times.

With thoughts of these students in mind, out-of-the-box leaders help the youngest boys and girls make gingerbread houses during Parent Day at the Early Childhood Center. Out-of-the-box leaders bake cookies and participate in the creation of family platters. Out-of-the-box leaders sit in the front row for the first concert solo performed by a nervous student. They give the thumbs-up sign and go backstage to offer congratulations. Out-of-the-box leaders give a freshman student a ride home when the nurse indicates that the parent is unable to come to school to pick up the student. Out-of-the-box leaders sit on the floor during Family Day and listen to a young boy and girl read their story. Out-of-the-box leaders can be seen sitting in very small chairs and sharing lunch with students.

WORLD CAFÉ

Out-of-the-box leaders would like to teach the world to have meaningful conversations. They support community conversations about important issues and topics. They help facilitate small-group dialogue in large-group settings. They support the acquisition of appropriate furniture—small round tables and chairs—to support proven and effective dialogue strategies such as the "World Café."

CARING RELATIONSHIPS

If you think a lot about caring being at the heart or the center of a system, then you probably work in an organization where people depend a lot upon each other. Out-of-the-box leaders understand that schools are a set of complex and interdependent relationships. I believe that the more you care for and about others, the more rewarding, on a daily basis, will be your role of servant leader.

REFERENCE

Senge, P. (1994). *The fifth discipline fieldbook*. New York: Currency.

CHAPTER FOUR

AN EPISTEMOLOGICAL PROBLEM

What If We Have the Wrong Theory?

THOMAS J. SERGIOVANNI

I t is not that simple. Thinking about leadership "out of the box" requires us to explore the mindscapes and the epistemologies that routinely color our perceptions and create our realities. The world is not always what we think it is. This is because we get what we expect, and we expect what we believe to be true (see, for example, Sergiovanni, 1985; Siegel, 2006). One thing is certain. Changing our minds about the leadership theories and practices that we currently believe in and that we currently use is difficult. But this change has to come first, followed by an honest commitment to climb out of the box that now imprisons us. Unless we change what we believe, change our definition of effective practice, and change the purposes we want to be at the center of our work, there is little hope that *any* proposed change will succeed over time.

Karl Weick tells a story about a group of soldiers lost in the Alps after two days in a snowstorm (cited in Mintzberg, Ahlstrand, & Lampel, 1998, pp. 159–160). On the third day, the soldiers reappeared and explained, "At first we considered ourselves lost and waited for the end. Then one of us found a map in his pocket. That calmed us down. We pitched camp, waited out the snowstorm, and used the map to discover our bearings. And here we are." Their lieutenant examined this life-saving map and discovered, to his astonishment, that it was not a map of the Alps but a map of the Pyrenees! (Weick, 1995, p. 54).

As Weick (1990) explains, "With the map in hand, no matter how crude it is, people encode what they see to conform as closely as possible to what is on the map. The map prefigures their perceptions, and they see what they expect to see" (p. 5).

Mindscapes operate like maps. They shape our perceptions so that we see what we expect to see. Unnoticed, our mindscapes frame the way we think and then provide us with a rationale for legitimizing our thoughts and actions. Mindscapes are difficult to escape from. Figuring out ways to help leaders break out of them is an important step in bringing about change.

————————— ✀ —————————

Mindscapes are difficult to escape from. Figuring out ways to help leaders break out of them is an important step in bringing about change.

Epistemologies are like mindscapes that operate on a larger scale, often shaping a worldview strong enough for many people to share. When several people work together to promote, refine, and extend a worldview, they function as a community of practice. By paying attention to mindscapes and epistemologies, and by knowing ourselves better, we can free ourselves from their influence and see reality for what it really is.

Improving schools is not as easy as it sounds. Hanging onto improvements once they are in place is even more difficult. Our difficulties in both cases may be the result of using the wrong theories of leadership and the wrong theories of school improvement. No matter how good our intentions, and no matter how hard we try to change things for the better, *wrong theories equal wrong practices.* Things wouldn't be so bad if we only had mindscape problems. Mindscape problems resemble spring thunderstorms. But we have epistemological problems, too—and epistemological problems resemble summer hurricanes.

Thus, two hurricane thoughts are important. The first thought is this: What will happen if we only look ahead for answers, neglecting our history? Will we make the same mistakes over and over again? For many, thinking "out of the box" requires that we look forward to find the questions and answers that can help us think anew about schools and their improvement. But we should look to the past as well. In our eagerness to succeed, we created the box from which we now seek to escape. But the answers will not be found in new visions that ignore where we have been, that ignore what we already know about creating great schools.

In this chapter, I rely on the seminal ideas of several organizational theorists from the past, whose work still influences the way we think about leadership and school improvement. Two theorists in particular are Peter Blau and Richard Scott, whose classic 1962 book, *Formal Organizations: A Comparative Approach,* proposed that some organizations are best understood as *social* rather than *formal.* Formal and social organizations are conceptually grounded in different epistemologies. If we have the wrong epistemology for the school, we will have a flawed practice—a theme I will soon develop further.

———————— ⚜ ————————

No matter how good our intentions, and no matter how hard we try to change things for the better, wrong theories equal wrong practices.

I rely also on the work of Philip Selznick as presented in his influential book, *Leadership in Administration: A Sociological Interpretation,* first published in 1957, with a later edition in 1984. Selznick proposed a theory of administration and organization that relies on his "institutional" perspective. He provides answers to the questions, How do organizations become institutions, and why is it important for them (schools, for example) to do so?

In sum, Blau and Scott proposed that social organizations are a better organizing alternative than formal organizations for some kinds of entities—families and schools, for instance. Similarly, Selznick proposed transforming some organizations into *institutions,* as an alternative to retaining their identity as formal organizations. In both cases, we in the education community chose to refuse these offers. We were determined to go forward as formal organizations no matter how flawed this epistemology may be for schools.

The second hurricane thought asks, How can we be more effective leaders if we do not have the right theory? But I'm getting ahead of myself. The principle *wrong theory equals wrong practice* may hit the nail on the head, but we need to hit harder to find meanings and understandings that will help us become different leaders. If we are at all serious about changing our practice, we will have to accept the fact that, for many leaders, nothing short of a transformation in their theories and practices will be required.

EPISTEMOLOGIES ARE KEY

Epistemology is a branch of philosophy concerned with the origin, nature, methods, and limits of human knowledge. Epistemologies are coherent bodies of knowledge that include beliefs and frameworks that are used to create meanings and to create realities. Different bodies of knowledge, beliefs, and frameworks create different meanings and realities.

As we shall soon see, the epistemologies that dominate the development, creation, and use of knowledge in school leadership and school improvement reflect a set of assumptions, beliefs, and ways of knowing that are at the core of our bureaucratic, corporate society. The underlying framework is that of the school as a formal organization. An alternative underlying framework is the school as a social organization. Viewed as social organizations, schools can resemble communities, congregations, and families. These differing epistemologies reflect the training we as educators receive; the ways in which we master our craft; and the basic assumptions, understandings, and realities that color what we see—and do not see.

In brief, we are trapped by the boxes we live in, the boxes we believe in, and the boxes we use to create designs and to develop our practice. Developing new and more effective leadership designs and school improvement strategies requires making deeply rooted changes that result in breaking away from existing values and ideas. *This is the new challenge of leadership and the new challenge of change.*

As we plan our breakout, two questions need to be addressed. First, how do we get out? Second, once out, where do we go next? I suggest that we begin by looking to the past, to the many lost opportunities to create great schools—schools where students routinely achieve at high levels; schools that know what their purposes are, take those purposes seriously as pathways to their goals, and use them as benchmarks for gauging success. Great schools are routinely responsive to the needs of students, teachers, and families. By contrast, today's schools too frequently borrow and use generic organizational and managerial frameworks to pursue look-alike schooling.[1] But generic organizational and managerial frameworks will not work well in today's school environment.

Why not? Because school leadership and school improvement are relatively weak sciences. Weak sciences lead to the development of second-tier practices. Thus, very few ideas about school leadership and about school improvement are home-born and -grown. Instead of originating in the school, they are borrowed from other disciplines with stronger epistemologies. The stronger a field's epistemology, the more that field is able to develop its own practices. Weak fields have difficulty pushing ahead to new ground. Because weak fields can't go it alone and must rely on excessive borrowing, they look to other fields for new knowledge and new practices. Whether or not this knowledge fits the school is another question, but good fits are rare.

Today's schools too frequently borrow and use generic organizational and managerial frameworks to pursue look-alike schooling.

QUESTIONS OF VALIDITY

Pages and pages of analysis and advice about the discipline and practice of educational administration are stored away in the world's libraries. But the questions we must answer again and again are, What if we have the wrong theory? and What if our theory of educational administration is not valid? Validity depends on the cogency and relevance of our theories and practices. Cogency and relevance are the basic standards in science for determining what is true, and what should be done as a result.

A major problem is that existing conceptions of organizations and of leadership, when applied to schools, are neither cogent nor relevant—and thus may be invalid. A valid practice would require that we change our conception of schools from one that believes them to be formal organizations to one that sees them as social organizations.[2] Moving in this direction will require that we change our emphasis from a leadership practice based on bureaucratic and personal authority to one based on moral authority. These changes, I argue, will make our theories and practices more cogent and relevant. To this end, I propose a cognitive approach to leadership based on the moral authority of ideas, values, and purposes rather than on the bureaucratic authority of hierarchies and the personal authority of personalities. *This stance helps us understand schools as moral communities.*

SCHOOL LEADERSHIP AND THE TYPE IV ERROR

Let me begin by discussing cogency and relevance within the context of four types of error that can be made in scientific theory and research:

- Type I Error, misjudged cogency: an error in judgment that results when standards are set too high
- Type II Error, misjudged cogency: an error in judgment that results when standards are set too low
- Type III Error, misplaced cogency: an error in judgment that results when the wrong problem is addressed regardless of cogency of method
- Type IV Error, misplaced relevance: an error in judgment that results when cogent knowledge (which is relevant for one kind of problem but not for another) is applied to the problem for which it is not relevant

For the purpose of this discussion, I will focus only on the last type: misplaced relevance. Misplaced relevance refers to the development and use of cogent knowledge that is relevant to one type of problem but not to another. When this happens, we commit the Type IV Error (Dunn, 1980, p. 39). Using cogent knowledge borrowed from the world of formal organizations to help distribute resources in a family setting is one example. Within formal organizations, resources are usually distributed based on merit. The best producers get more resources than do their less productive neighbors. In the typical family, by contrast, the distribution of resources is not so much based on merit as on need. New shoes go to the child with the greatest need, regardless of his or her performance in fulfilling household chores. Should the family decide to give new shoes to a child based on merit rather than need, a Type IV Error would be made and eyebrows would be raised. A Type IV Error is also made when leaders remind their constituents that we must feed students so that they will be better able to learn, as in, "You can't learn on an empty stomach." Perhaps, but the overarching reason for feeding students should be that they are hungry.

When the Type IV Error is made in schools, it involves cogent knowledge that, for example, may be relevant for the corporate world or may be relevant for some other kind of formal organization but is not relevant for social organizations. When we use this knowledge anyway, we are using the wrong theory—and the wrong theory equals the wrong practice.

How Formal and Social Organizations Differ

I argue that one of the problems we face in trying to improve schools is that they are organized and operate as if they are formal organizations. This generic view allows for easy transfer to the school of assumptions and practices that have been found to work elsewhere.[3] Thus, strategies for change that work well in the corporate world and in other sectors of our society are generally assumed to apply to the school (Sergiovanni, 1996). This is why the images of corporate restructuring—downsizing, standards setting, accountability, and increased competition—play such a large role in school reform efforts. This is also why images from other sectors of our society—the worlds of civic and social enterprises, such as families, faith communities, volunteer groups, and mutual aid societies—are often overlooked. Most experts in organizational theory, however, do not agree with the view that all organizations are the same. Instead they take the view that formal organizations represent only one of several ways in which humans organize themselves and relate to each other.

Blau and Scott (1962) noted clearly that their book was written for those interested in formal organizations and was not relevant

Strategies for change that work well in the corporate world and in other sectors of our society are generally assumed to apply to the school.

for social organizations. Thus, using this cogent and appealing book in schools is an example of one of the most serious mistakes we have made as we have selected books and ideas for use in educational administration over the years. And since the wrong theory equals the wrong practice, we are still making the same mistakes.

In Blau and Scott's words, "we would not call a family an organization [meaning formal organization], nor would we so designate a friendship clique, or a community"(p. 2). To them, what differentiates formal organizations from more social enterprises is how human conduct is socially organized. In social organizations, the structure of social relations and the shared beliefs and orientations that unite members and guide their conduct are important. Blau and Scott refer to these dimensions as networks of social relations or shared orientations. The dimensions are similar to community concepts such as social structure and culture. The DNA of social organizations is their *lifeworld.* Social organizations thrive when their lifeworlds drive the systemsworld; they suffer when the systemsworld drives the lifeworld (two terms that are taken from the work of Habermas, 1987). The systemsworld provides the system of means and other instrumentalities that schools need to help them achieve their purposes. The lifeworld includes the traditions, rituals, and norms that define a school's culture. If Blau and Scott and other experts in organizational theory are right and different types of organizations exist, then a more effective approach to changing schools may be to first identify the organizational type that best fits the school. We could then adopt an approach to understanding change that leads to the development of special change strategies for the school—change strategies that match the school's special leadership and cultural requirements.

The educational philosopher Kenneth Strike (2004) proposes that schools should be more like congregations than banks. Schools as congregations is a metaphor for schools as communities. Strike argues that schools as communities should be rooted in a shared "educational product," vision, and language. The four C's of community he proposes are *c*oherence, *c*ohesion, *c*are, and *c*ontext.

To put it crisply, *the formal organization is the wrong epistemology for the school.* When the theories and practices suitable for formal organizations are used by the school anyway, things rapidly go from bad to worse. If you want to improve the school, use the theories and practices that apply to social organizations. Viewing schools as learning and caring communities helps.

INSTITUTIONAL LEADERSHIP AND ORGANIZATIONAL CHARACTER

The seeds for Blau and Scott's (1962) distinction between formal and social organization and for Strike's suggestion that schools be more like congregations than banks can be found in Philip Selznick's monumental 1957 work, *Leadership in Administration: A Sociological Interpretation.* In this book, Selznick compares "organizations" with "institutions," pointing out that institutions are more successful in providing for the needs of their members and in accomplishing purposes. Organizations are made up of standard building blocks that lend themselves to manipulation by administrators who are interchangeable across all organizations, and whose practice involves the use of generic theories, concepts, and skills. Their roles are generalized to the point that they become similar to parallel roles in other organizations. From an organizational perspective, successfully managing a shoe store, bank, insurance company, hospital, day-care center, church, school, or family all require the same insights, know-how, and skills. The consequence of adopting this generic approach is a lapse in integrity and a loss of character that lead to undifferentiated organizations and mediocre performance.

By contrast, institutions maintain integrity and character by being *unique in their purposes,* structures, and ways of doing things. They develop distinctive ways of making decisions, distinctive commitments to their purposes, distinctive ways of operating, and distinctive connections to the people they serve. In Selznick's (1957) words

> *If you want to improve the school, use the theories and practices that apply to social organizations. Viewing schools as learning and caring communities helps.*

In this way the organization as a technical instrument takes on values. As a vehicle of group integrity it becomes in some degree an end in itself. This process of becoming infused with value is part of what we mean by institutionalization. As this occurs, *organization management* becomes *institutional leadership.* . . . The building of integrity is part of what we have called the "institutional embodiment of purpose" and its protection is a major function of leadership. (pp. 138–139)

Becoming an institution and being infused with value would mean that schools know what their purposes are, believe in these purposes, and use them to develop frameworks for action that become benchmarks for formative evaluation and for professional development. "Where institutionalization is well advanced, distinctive outlooks, habits and other commitments are unified, coloring all aspects of organizational life and lending it a *social integration* that goes well beyond formal co-ordination and command" (Selznick, 1957, p. 40).

Selznick's theory of institutional leadership provides a major breakthrough in understanding the way organizations and institutions work; it has much to contribute to the way schools should be viewed. Institutional leadership seeks to bring integrity to an enterprise, and to transform the enterprise from an organization to an institution. As the process of institutionalization occurs, schools evolve away from generic organizations and become distinctive communities. As community evolves, the school not only comes to develop a distinctive character, but a distinctive competence as well.

THE RETREAT TO MEANS AND THE LOSS OF PURPOSING

To be an effective institutional leader, one must have a reasonable amount of control over goals and purposes—not just the means to achieve them. This configuration allows the leader to reach deeply into his or her organization and into the community, tapping what is known and then aggregating it so that the school itself becomes smarter. *Interpersonal* leaders focus on building up *personal* authority as the basis for their leadership. *Institutional* leaders focus on building up *moral* authority as the basis for their leadership. As Selznick (1957) explains

> Finally, the role of the institutional leader should be clearly distinguished from that of the "interpersonal" leader. The latter's task is to smooth the path of human interaction, ease communication, evoke personal devotion and allay anxiety. His expertness has relatively little to do with content; he is more concerned with persons than with policies. His main contribution is to the efficiency of the enterprise. The institutional leader, on the other

hand, *is primarily an expert in the promotion and protection of values.* (pp. 27–28)

Harvard Business School Professor Abraham Zaleznik (1989) believes that the failure of management is a result of the substitution of process for substance. Under these circumstances, leadership becomes vacuous. Schools come to stand for less and less, and their character is placed at risk. The importance of management processes to school effectiveness should not be underestimated, but such processes are not substitutes for substance. It is important, for example, to know how to get from point A to point B, and sound management can help; however, the substance of administrative leadership is concerned with such questions as whether B is better than A and why, and how our culture will be strengthened as a result of getting there. Substance defines who we are and what values are important to us. Substance leads to ends. Process provides frameworks for achieving our goals. Process leads to means. As we retreat to means, we face the loss of purposing.

IDEA-BASED LEADERSHIP

Few issues are more important to leadership than deciding what will be the reasons why others are being asked to follow.[4] Many will respond to that question as follows: "Follow me because of my position in the school and the system of roles, expectations, and rules that I represent." This reliance on bureaucratic authority is the simplest and the most direct way to get things done in schools.

An alternative response might be, "Follow me because I will make it worthwhile if you do." This is perhaps the most popular way to get things done in a school: Rely on personal authority. Personal authority is expressed in the form of the leader's charisma, motivational abilities, and human relations skills.

Bureaucratic authority takes the form of mandates, rules, regulations, policies, job descriptions, and expectations communicated by leaders and others. When leaders base their practice on *bureaucratic* authority, teachers are expected to

When leaders base their practice on bureaucratic *authority, teachers are expected to respond appropriately or face the consequences.*

respond appropriately or face the consequences. When leaders base their practice on *personal* authority, teachers are supposed to respond to their personality and to the pleasant environment that they provide by behaving appropriately.

Few readers would advocate a leadership based primarily on bureaucratic authority; however, the primacy of leadership based on personal authority remains popular. Leaders like to think of themselves as being good motivators who know how to handle people. But following a leader because of his or her personality or interpersonal skills is really a poor reason. Teachers ought to follow their principals, for example, not because they are clever manipulators but because these leaders stand for something, are persons of substance, and base their practice on ideas.

When purposes are in place and shared values are cultivated, an idea framework evolves that encourages teachers to respond to a sense of obligation to embody these ideas in their behavior. A moral authority emerges that compels them to participate in shared commitments and to be connected to others with whom these commitments are shared.

If school leaders commit to ideas as their primary source of authority and make ideas central to their practice, then they are free from worrying so much about all of the behavioral nuances that must be considered under other approaches to leadership. Further, idea-based leadership communicates to teachers that they are respected, autonomous, committed, capable, and morally responsible adults— adult professionals who are able to join with the leader in a common commitment to making things in the school work better for children. Unfortunately, getting leaders to rely on idea-based leadership is often a hard sell.

THEORIES FOR THE SCHOOL

Bureaucratic, rules-based leadership and personality-based leadership are embedded in three theories for the school that shape the way we think about school leadership, organization, and management: the pyramid theory, the railroad theory, and the high-performance system theory. Below I provide a thumbnail sketch of each.

At the end of this discussion, I will propose *school as moral community* as an alternative theory. Leadership in this theory is idea-based; the theory of organization used is social rather than formal. Further, the transformation of the school from formal organization to institution is the fundamental strategy underlying theories of action. Wrong theory equals wrong practice is a worry for leaders of the school as moral community. Consequently, the climate and culture are constantly monitored to ensure that social organization, institutionalization, and leadership by ideas are alive and well.

Pyramid Theory

The pyramid theory assumes that the way to control the work of others is to have one person assume responsibility by providing directions, supervision, and inspection. But as the number of people to be supervised increases, and as separate work sites develop, management burdens must be delegated to others, and a hierarchical system emerges. Rules and regulations are developed to ensure that all of the managers think and act the same way; these provide the protocols and guidelines used for planning, organizing, and directing (see, for example, Mintzberg, 1979).

Railroad Theory

The railroad theory assumes that the way to control the work of people who have different jobs and who work in different locations is by standardizing the work processes. Instead of relying on direct supervision and hierarchical authority, a great deal of time is spent anticipating all the questions and problems that are likely to arise. Then answers and solutions are developed that represent tracks people must follow to get from one goal or outcome to another. Once the tracks are laid, all that needs to be done is to train people how to follow them, and to set up monitoring systems to be sure that they are followed (Mintzberg, 1979).

The railroad theory, applied to schools, creates an instructional delivery system in which specific objectives are identified and tightly aligned to an explicit curriculum and a specific method of teaching. Teachers are supervised and evaluated, and students tested, to ensure that the approved curriculum and teaching scripts are being followed. Administrators and teachers use fewer skills, and both teacher and student work becomes increasingly standardized.

High-Performance System Theory

The high-performance system theory differs from the others by *de-emphasizing* both top-down hierarchies and detailed scripts that tell people what to do. Decentralization is key, with workers empowered to make their own decisions about *how* to do things. One gets control by connecting people to outcomes rather than rules or work scripts. High-performance system theory assumes that the key to effective leadership is to connect workers tightly to ends, but only loosely to means (see, for example, Peters & Waterman, 1982).

When the high-performance system theory is applied to schools, the ends are measurable learning outcomes that are usually stated as standards. Though outcomes are standardized, schools are free to decide how they are going to achieve them. Administrators and teachers can organize schools and teach in ways that they think will best enable them to meet the standards. High-performance system theory emphasizes collecting data to determine how well workers are doing, and to improve the likelihood that standardized outcomes specified by distant authorities are met.

While the pyramid, railroad, and high-performance system theories provide understandings that can help us make better decisions about school leadership, they also share features that make their systematic application to schools inappropriate. In all three theories, schools are perceived as formal organizations. (High-performance system theory is often a less rigid version.)

This separation of what will be done and how it will be done from the actual doing may work in running a chain of fast-food restaurants, but not for schools, in which professional discretion is essential to success.

Both the pyramid and railroad theories separate the planning of how work will be done from its actual performance. "Managers" (state and other distant authorities) are responsible for planning *what* will be done and *how* it will be done. "Workers" (principals, teachers, and students) are responsible for *doing.* This separation of what will be done and how it will be done from the actual doing may work in running a chain of fast-food restaurants, but not for schools, in which professional discretion is essential to success.

In high-performance system theory, workers are provided with outcomes and other standards; they then get to decide how to do the work necessary for the outcomes and standards to be achieved. But because planning what to do is separated from planning how to do it, problems of isolation, fragmentation, and loss of meaning remain. When means and ends are separated, not only is professional discretion compromised, but so are democratic principles. Few parents, principals, teachers, or students are likely to feel empowered by being involved in decision making processes that are limited to issues of how, but not what—of means, but not ends.

THE SCHOOL AS A MORAL COMMUNITY

Many school leaders don't ignore the three theories, but they don't put much stock in them either. Instead, they view schools as moral communities and struggle to make this view a reality. A moral community has two important advantages over the other theories: It provides for moral connections among teachers, heads, parents, and students, and it advocates helping all of them to become self-managing.

All theories of leadership emphasize connecting people to each other and to their work. These connections satisfy the needs for coordination and commitment that any enterprise must meet to be successful. The work of teachers, for example, must fit together in some sensible way if school purposes are to be realized, and teachers must be motivated to do whatever is necessary in order to make this connection.

But not all theories emphasize the same kinds of connections. The pyramid, railroad, and high-performance system theories emphasize contractual connections and assume that people are primarily motivated by self-interest. To get things done, extrinsic or intrinsic rewards are traded for compliance, and penalties are traded for noncompliance. Leadership inevitably takes the form of bartering between the leader and the led.

Moral connections are stronger than the connections that come from extrinsic or intrinsic rewards. They are grounded in cultural norms rather than in psychological needs. "A norm . . . is an idea in the minds of the members of a group, an idea that can be put in the form of a statement specifying

Moral connections are stronger than the connections that come from extrinsic or intrinsic rewards. They are grounded in cultural norms rather than in psychological needs.

what the members . . . should do, ought to do, are expected to do, under given circumstances" (Homans, 1950, p. 123). A norm is a norm only when not following it leads to some kind of sanction or penalty. Usually, this penalty takes the form of feeling uneasy when we are not meeting commitments or when important others are disappointed with what we are doing.

With leadership firmly grounded in shared ideas, and with moral connections in place, administrators, teachers, parents, and students can come together in a shared followership. The leader serves as head follower by leading the discussion about what is worth following and by modeling, teaching, and helping others to become better followers. When this happens, the emphasis changes from direct leadership based on rules and personality, to a different kind of leadership aimed in the direction of stewardship and service and based on ideas.

SOME RECOMMENDATIONS

All of us want to develop new leadership values and practices that are more valuable and more effective than those we now use. If we are successful, we will be able to establish a beachfront of practices that are out of the box! But there are complexities. In this chapter, I have called attention to epistemological problems that must be resolved first if we are going to move successfully to new ground.

In schools today, we are presently committing the Type IV Error. When relevance is misplaced, this error becomes increasingly common. As mentioned earlier, misplaced relevance is an error in judgment that results when cogent knowledge—relevant for one kind of problem but not another—is used for the other anyway. For example, certain values, purposes, and practices that are appropriate for formal organizations such as the corporation, but not for social organizations such as families or schools, are applied to family and schools anyway. Formal organizations and institutions work the same way. It is the institutional epistemology that fits the school.

How serious is the problem? The dangerous consequence is that we will wind up using the wrong practices. Earlier I proposed that the school as moral community is a metaphor better suited to the school than the pyramid, the railroad, or the high-performance system. This alternative relies on leading with ideas and views moral authority as the source for making decisions. There is much more to say about this topic, and even more to do if we want to avoid the Type IV Error. My hope is that others will join the conversation and that the issues I raise here will be pursued by students of school leadership and improvement. To this end, I conclude by proposing some recommendations for your consideration.

1. Launch a massive effort to close the gap between what we know and what we see in too many schools. Virtually every important practice can be found to be alive and well in some school, somewhere. The key question is, how do we scale up so that these qualities become part of the ordinary lives of all schools?

2. Provide coaching for school leaders, especially for superintendents and principals. In the end, it is the superintendent and principals who are responsible for providing the leadership that resolves epistemological questions. School leaders will be more effective change agents if they have help in navigating the complexities of reconciling the mindscapes they *have* with the mindscapes they *need* to help the school become an effective moral community.

3. Be sure that coaches are able to provide help in dealing with three kinds of questions:

   Content questions such as, What are our purposes? What are we trying to accomplish? How will what teachers and administrators actually do in the classrooms and the school change? What effects will we seek in student achievement? Do we have a balanced assessment portfolio that includes indicators other than just test scores?

   Process questions such as, How will we accomplish our goals? What means will we use to help teachers move along? How do we get commitment for change from teachers? How must we work together as members of communities of practice?

   Culture questions such as, What changes will we need to make in the norms system of our schools? What will be the accepted ways we do things? How will our purposes, values, and commitments be used to point the way to evaluate our work? (Neufield & Roper, 2003; Sergiovanni & Starratt, in press).

4. Bring together the high-performance system theory and the school as moral community into one integrated theory. There is a place for pluralism. But there is also a place for coherence, and neither the high-performance system theory nor the school as moral community is strong enough to go it alone. Any breakout from the box will not be sustained unless it is part of a larger and more powerful effort.[5]

5. Rein in the visionaries. You can't do without visionary leadership. But you can have too much of it. When you have too much, it becomes a hardship for people with different visions to get together, to help each other, and to join forces in understanding the theories and practices that make up school leadership and improvement. It is *craftspeople* who make the worlds of school leadership and school improvement go around. Craftspeople know how to turn visions into realities, how to take big ideas and make them understandable and useful, and how to bring together the right mix of human resources to make schools work well. Let visionaries sketch out the big picture. Let visionaries help us to see what is possible—and craftspeople will then work to change these visions into realities. Craftspeople like to view leadership as a design practice that transfers ideas into things.

Let visionaries sketch out the big picture. Let visionaries help us to see what is possible—and craftspeople will then work to change these visions into realities.

6. Adopt leadership with ideas as your primary leadership strategy. Leadership with ideas places process over substance and plays a key role in transforming schools into institutions. Ideas often take the form of promises. When we make a public commitment to ideas that define who we are and what we are trying to accomplish, we are in essence promising to embody these ideas in our practice. We now have a responsibility to meet our commitments. These characteristics result in the school becoming a community of responsibility. Ideas are a powerful substitute for leadership. The more firmly we have ideas in place, the less we need active leadership.

NOTES

1. There are many, many exceptions. Included are schools that function successfully as social organizations; schools that have transformed themselves into institutions; schools where leading with ideas is routine; schools that function as moral communities; and schools that are communities of practice. Adlai Stevenson High School in Lincolnshire, Illinois, is one well-known example of a school that has transformed itself from an organization into an institution and one that serves as a model of a social organization in action. Still, Richard DuFour, an important figure in the transformation of Stevenson, tells me that too many visitors to Stevenson adopt the right practices without changing their mindscapes or epistemologies (personal communication, November 2004). Regardless of appearances, these visitors remain in the box. There is an important lesson here. The challenge is that if we want real change—change that will sustain itself over time—we will have to go beyond first-level changes and second-level changes to changes in the epistemology of the school itself.

2. As suggested above, I am proposing that the school be thought of as a community, which is one kind of social organization. Examples of formal organizations are corporations, armies, unions, and hospitals. Examples of social organizations are families, friendship cliques, and communities (see, for example, Blau & Scott, 1962; for a more recent discussion of formal and social organizations, see Strike, 2004). Philip Selznick's (1957) understanding of schools and other organizations as being transformed into institutions will be discussed later in the chapter.

3. This discussion of formal organizations and social organizations follows closely that which appears in Sergiovanni (2000, pp. 151–153).

4. This discussion of idea-based leadership and theories of schooling follows closely Sergiovanni (2001, pp. 28–35).

5. As a member in good standing of the school as moral community "club," I too am captured by a specific epistemology—one that I will have to let go of if we are to bring together high-performance system and school as moral community theories.

REFERENCES

Blau, P. M., & Scott, W. R. (1962). *Formal organizations: A comparative approach.* San Francisco: Chandler.

Dunn, W. N. (1980, June 18–20). *Reform as argument. international conference on political realization of social science knowledge and research: Toward two scenarios.* Paper presented at the Conference of the Institute for Advanced Studies, Vienna, Austria.

Habermas, J. (1987). *The theory of communicative action. Vol. 2: Lifeworld and system: A critique of functional reason* (T. McCarthy, Trans.). Boston: Beacon Press.

Homans, G. C. (1950). *The human group.* New York: Harcourt Brace.

Mintzberg, H. (1979.) *The structuring of organizations.* Englewood Cliffs, NJ: Prentice Hall.

Mintzberg, H, Ahlstrand, B., & Lampel, J. (1998). *Strategy safari: A guided tour through the wilds of strategic management.* New York: Free Press.

Neufield, B., & Roper, D. (2003, June). Coaching: A strategy for developing instructional capacity. Paper co-published by Aspen Institute Program on Education and Annenberg Institute for School Reform, p. 3.

Peters, T. J., & Waterman, R. H., Jr. (1982). *In search of excellence.* New York: Harper & Row.

Selznick, P. (1957). *Leadership in administration: A sociological interpretation.* Evanston, IL: Harper & Row.

Sergiovanni, T. J. (1985, Fall). Landscapes, mindscapes, and reflective practice in supervision and evaluation. *Journal of Curriculum and Supervision, 1*(1), 5–18.

Sergiovanni, T. J. (1996). *Leadership for the schoolhouse: How is it different? Why is it important?* San Francisco: Jossey-Bass.

Sergiovanni, T. J. (2000). *The lifeworld of leadership: Creating culture, community, and personal meaning in our schools.* San Francisco: Jossey-Bass.

Sergiovanni, T. J. (2001). *Leadership: What's in it for schools?* London: Routledge Falmer.

Sergiovanni, T. J., & Starratt, R. J. (in press). *Supervision: A redefinition* (8th ed.). New York: McGraw-Hill.

Siegel, H. (2006). Epistemological diversity and educational research: Much ado about nothing much? *Educational Researcher, 35*(2), 3–12.

Strike, K. A. (2004). Community, the missing element of school reform: Why schools should be more like congregations than banks. *American Journal of Education, 110*(3).

Weick, K. E. (1990). Cartographic myths in organizations. In A. S. Huff (Ed.), *Mapping strategic thought* (pp. 1–10). New York: Wiley.

Weick, K. E. (1995). *Sensemaking in organizations.* Thousand Oaks, CA: Sage.

Zaleznik, A. (1989). *The managerial mystique: Restoring leadership in business.* New York: Harper & Row.

CHAPTER FIVE

REFLECTIONS ON LEADERSHIP

When Hearts and Minds Are Open

KARI COCOZZELLA AND
THOMAS J. KASPER

A warm December sun filtered through the large windows of the coffee shop, dancing across the tiny corner table. But the two people making their way toward the nook scarcely noticed the sun, or the other patrons in the busy store.

"This is just the right place to talk!" Kari exclaimed. Indeed, it was the perfect place to engage in a passionate discussion about what it takes to be an effective school leader in a challenging and often politically charged school environment, surrounded every day with issues of accountability and ever-higher standards.

"How many times do people get the opportunity to meet and talk about how deep-rooted, gut-wrenching personal beliefs shape what they think and do every day?" Tom commented. His gray eyes sparkled with enthusiasm as he sat down with a steaming mug of coffee.

"Not often enough," Kari agreed. She immediately felt a sense of relief. Tom seemed full of energy for what he did on a daily basis in his work as a school leader. She had first met him at a leadership conference two years earlier. Now they were colleagues, charged with trying to communicate the essence of their work to other school leaders. It was a daunting task, but one that both were committed to doing.

Within minutes, the world retreated as their conversation focused on what it takes to participate in and create multiple levels of leadership. This kind of focus has to be present in order to build and sustain a school where individuals take collective responsibility for enabling and supporting the conditions in which everyone— students and teachers alike—can feel successful, challenged, and valued. If teachers, support staff, and parents are an integral part of an environment where such deep discussions are a visible part of the daily routine, students will reap the benefits.

Tom seemed to sense Kari's initial reluctance to share, so he jumped in: "Some teachers in my district attended a leadership conference where you were presenting, and brought back some materials and handouts on building a pyramid of interventions. I told them that I met you last winter at a conference in Sedona, Arizona."

"I remember!" Kari nodded. "We had a conversation out by the pool after the day's events and started talking about being an effective principal and discussing what 'effective' means and looks like."

Time seemed to stand still as Tom and Kari shared thoughts, feelings, beliefs, wonderings, and passion for "what can be." The conversation leaned toward the concept of *being* a leader rather than *doing* leadership.

"What's the difference?" Kari asked, and her question opened the floodgates. The two principals spent the next hour picking each other's brains, trying to get a handle on how leadership happens and how its effects flow throughout an organization. Soon, a wealth of anecdotes and stories about their schools, their personal beliefs, and foundational knowledge began to yield several significant themes to investigate. Thoughts were thrown out for discussion, churned around, discarded, and revisited. What finally emerged was the identification of some core values that guide effective leadership practices.

I truly believe that our purpose is to help students acquire academic and social skills in order to have a meaningful and successful life.

"Okay, how would you describe an effective leader?" Kari asked Tom, really wanting to hear his perspective. In her heart, she knew that this was the critical question. This was it. The rest of the conversation would either be a debate or an ebb and flow of bits and pieces of insight and reflection.

Tom glanced down, placed his chin in his right hand, elbow on the table, and thought for a moment before responding. "My own leadership style revolves around thinking in terms of other people and the larger purpose outside of myself."

"Can you give me an example of what that looks like?" Kari probed.

"I think the success of my school doesn't only fall on my shoulders or rely on my determination of what needs to be done," Tom replied. "I truly believe that our purpose is to help students acquire academic and social skills in order to have a meaningful and successful life. I believe that teachers are in the best position to know what they and their students can best benefit from."

Kari wanted to know more. "What have your teachers done recently to accept that responsibility and to take control of their own learning and access the expertise of others in your school?"

"Here's what we did last Wednesday after school," Tom volunteered. Feeling the enthusiasm in his voice, Kari picked up her pencil, guessing that he would be sharing a simple idea, but one that would strongly reflect the larger idea of teachers taking control of their own learning in order to affect the learning of their own students.

"It seems like a small thing," Tom continued. "A group of teachers chose to study writing, others decided to investigate strategies to help reluctant learners, and still another group wanted to dialogue about reading comprehension strategies. Teachers determined their area of study based on the evidence from their students' work. They chose what was currently meaningful to them. I didn't decide for them. Yet it was understood that this time was about adult learning and how it connects to fostering student learning and achievement."

"What was your role in this?"

"My role was to help support teachers in their pursuits. I believe deeply that when we author something ourselves, it leads to long-term commitment and embeds itself into daily practice. I visited groups as an interested observer and participant, not to direct what or how they learned. I was a learner with them."

"Is this what you were thinking when we first mentioned *being* a leader rather than *doing* leadership?" Kari asked.

"Yes! Because I was demonstrating to them through my actions what it means to take responsibility for my own learning rather than directing them to what I think that they should learn."

"I think beliefs are transparent through one's actions. What did you do?"

Tom went on, "To indicate my support for them, I knew they needed resources, which included time. I worked to figure out a way to provide whatever was requested. For example, the fourth- and fifth-grade teachers needed texts for their book study and opportunities to be released from their classrooms in order to visit other classrooms. We were able to provide coverage from within the building or from outside with substitutes. Having said this, a deep belief of mine is that teachers benefit when they have knowledge of and use the tools to hold professional conversations. This includes building new structures and removing obstacles to achieve this end."

A deep belief of mine is that teachers benefit when they have knowledge of and use the tools to hold professional conversations. This includes building new structures and removing obstacles to achieve this end.

Kari thought for a moment. It takes skill and a commitment to having a focused and meaningful conversation. Tom must have done something to establish trust and respect among his staff.

"As I listened to teachers over the summer and again at the beginning of school last fall, I heard them overwhelmingly talk about the kind of school they wanted to be a part of," Tom continued. "They told me about wanting to be a part of a collaborative culture, tapping into the expertise that was already at their school, and needing and wanting the freedom to take risks without penalty. I knew I needed to restructure time and how we formally met, but also how we would meet on an informal level. Intuitively, I knew this meant not just being in the same room, but 'meeting' emotionally, intellectually, and with our hearts and souls."

"How did your actions show that you were demonstrating trust and respect for those given the huge responsibility of either making or breaking a child's spirit?" Kari asked. She had grappled with this question for some time, so she was extremely interested in Tom's thoughts.

"If we were going to truly 'meet,' I felt it was important to offer strategies for teachers to learn structured conversation protocols and ways that honored teachers' time and expertise," Tom replied. "We spent time learning facilitation skills in order to bring all voices into their conversations, to quiet those who tend to 'suck the air' out of the discussion, and to create the conditions that would enable people to experience fundamental shifts of mind in relation to how they view their work."

"What I hear, Tom, is that you had the wisdom to create multiple informal and formal opportunities to talk with and listen to your staff. I also notice that you seem to understand the critical importance of respecting where the teachers have been, where they are today, and where they might want to go as people and professionals. Basically, it seems to me that you honored their past, claimed their present, and had an unyielding hope for the future. Tell me, though," and here Kari paused for a moment, "what did you do when the 'tough stuff' reared its ugly head?"

"Well, that's just it," Tom said immediately, "because we started learning not to bury our heads in the sand over tough issues. We began to acknowledge that struggles and disagreements exist. We also acknowledged that, to a degree, struggles are born in our own heads based on how we think things should be and from our past experiences. To counter that, when we come to our groups now that we have learned how to talk with each other, we recognize that everyone has a piece to bring, some understanding to gain—and frankly, that they will inquire of each other and advocate for what is best for students. It's amazing what can be accomplished when we put issues on the table and we're willing to listen to and respect each other. Because we have felt so much success with each other when we interact this way, our conversations with *parents* have also become much more productive! Parents now see us as listeners and problem solvers with them when searching for ways to best support their children."

As Tom went to get a refill on his coffee, Kari sat back in the cushioned chair and felt an unbelievable sense of connection. This was so encouraging and energizing! She quickly jotted down some key words and phrases that seemed to encompass their conversation so far:

We started learning not to bury our heads in the sand over tough issues. We began to acknowledge that struggles and disagreements exist.

Respect   Reflect

Listen   Face the "tough stuff"

Empower	Energize
Trust	Share leadership
Collaborate	Credit wisdom (personal and collective)
Use intuition	Honor the past, be in the present, hope for the future

The once-empty coffee shop had filled with eager customers, clamoring to acquire their morning boost of caffeine. The sounds and smells of the coffee shop filled the air; jovial conversations bounced off the walls. The barista cheerfully greeted each person, seeming to know each customer's order even before it was placed. The second barista worked efficiently beside the first, quickly and accurately filling each order. Kari watched the interaction for a few moments and realized that both young women behind the espresso bar were demonstrating a perfect example of clear communication, knowledge of craft, and the development of relationships in order to successfully produce an end result. Suddenly she realized that the essence of leadership is not giving things or even providing visions. It is offering oneself and one's spirit!

When Tom returned, he noticed the enthusiastic expression on Kari's face and immediately wanted to find out what had happened.

"Okay, it looks as though you just won the lottery,' he prompted her. "What gives?"

"Watch the interactions between the two baristas and their customers." Tom turned in his chair to get a better view, watched for a few minutes, and then turned back to his companion. "They have great rapport with their customers, don't they?" he observed.

"And they work seamlessly together," Kari added.

"So that's the question, isn't it?" Tom asked. "How do relationship, rapport, and communication help us identify and understand our purpose, then enable us to carry out the mission and vision of an organization? It seems to me that the people working here understand the importance of cooperation and connectedness in order to meet their needs and the needs of their customers."

"Right." Kari continued, voicing her thoughts, "I think it's also incredibly important to make sure that everyone understands the purpose of the organization and has an opportunity to be involved in creating what it stands for. In my school, we have worked diligently together to write a clear mission, vision, and values that encapsulated our ideals and beliefs about how to make sure that every child had every opportunity to succeed. I'm not just talking about academic achievement. At our school, we recognize other traits, such as citizenship, being thoughtful, being productive, choosing a healthy lifestyle, and being ethical. We know these are also important to our children's success."

"There are two big ideas here that I think you've brought to the table," Tom interjected. "I'm curious about the process you used to create and clarify your school's mission, vision, and values. And I'd also like to know more about what you mean by 'other traits' and how this relates to success with children in a world that seems to place its primary value on academic achievement." Tom leaned in, prepared to listen intently.

"When I first started as a principal, I had a lot of theoretical knowledge," Kari recalled. "But I didn't know a lot about the nuts and bolts of actually putting that knowledge into practice. Luckily, I found a book on professional learning communities, written by Rick DuFour. I decided to take it to read while my 10-year-old son was at soccer practice. I brought my little blue lawn chair and diet soda, and sat far enough away from the action so I wouldn't get beaned by wayward soccer balls. As I started reading, I quickly became engrossed in the concepts of a professional learning community. Frustrated, I realized I had forgotten my yellow highlighter, so I began to dog-ear the most important pages. Pretty soon, I had to laugh, because I had turned down the corners of just about every page! This was great stuff! And it was written in a framework that was easily understood and very applicable. Soccer practice ended, yet I'd only read three chapters. Over the next couple of weeks, I kept reading, and formulating ideas in my head. I knew it would be critical to involve teachers in taking a look at the current mission of our school. I had not found a vision or values statement written down anywhere, though I knew both existed in spirit. I also knew I needed to acquire information from other stakeholders, such as parents, community members, and even students."

I think it's incredibly important to make sure that everyone understands the purpose of the organization and has an opportunity to be involved in creating what it stands for.

"A lot of this sounds like organizational learning to me," Tom reflected. "You know, where an organization comes together and determines what it needs collectively and what each must do personally in order to move forward to fully actualize its purpose."

"That's it," Kari smiled with appreciation. "Communication of expectations, purpose, mission, vision, and values must be clear to everyone and constantly embedded in everything we do, every conversation we have, and every decision we make. If not, frustration, lack of cohesiveness, anxiety, confusion, resistance, and inertia take over our best intentions. Everyone must be held accountable through vigilant monitoring by each other, not just by the identified leader."

"Kari, that sounds like a lot of theory again. How do you as a leader at your school apply this in your daily work? Tell me what you did when you worked on your mission, vision, and values."

Kari took a deep breath, slid off her shoes, and slipped them under the table. She tucked her feet off to the side, and pondered where to start.

"I spent a lot of time observing and watching people in action, going back to my office after the day was over and the children and teachers had left, filling pads of paper with reflections of what I had seen and heard throughout the day. What were teachers, parents, and students telling me through their actions? How could I access what was deepest in their hearts and souls? Because I knew it would be critical to infuse each person's spirit into the culture of the school. Armed with these questions, I set out to uncover the hidden, yet essential, understandings of what was important to those in the school. I decided to ask more explicit key questions of the school community. Here are some of the questions I asked:

1. I want my school to be a place where . . .

2. The kind of school I would like to teach in would . . .

3. What could we accomplish in the next five years that would make us proud?

4. What contributions can you make that will make our school the best it can be?

5. What do you need in order to be most effective and skilled in your work?

"What did you learn from the answers and what did you do with the information?" Tom encouraged Kari to continue.

"Well, it took some time," Kari admitted. "I compiled my information and shared it at various meetings—with the leadership, with the whole staff, with the PTA."

"It was a process, not an event," Tom said encouragingly.

"It sure was. I realized that it would be much better to carefully consider every thought, every belief, every idea, and to make sure to include *everyone* because it was *our* school, not *my* school. When I didn't get information back the first time from custodians, itinerant staff, and cafeteria staff, I went back and asked them personally for their ideas. I wanted them to know that every person, directly or indirectly, has a huge role in the education of our students and in the culture of the building. They looked surprised that I would be so persistent, but I felt that it was so important to include everyone. I wanted my actions to reflect my beliefs."

"I totally understand," Tom said. "In my first year at my previous school, I wanted to revisit the mission, vision, and values, but soon realized that I hadn't explicitly established relationships of trust with integrity. But I did plant the seeds to create opportunities for staff and community to express their views."

"What were the seeds?" Kari asked. "I'd really like to know because I may have done it differently. What works in one building isn't always as effective in another."

"In my case, because I had a veteran staff that had taken a lot of pride in building the culture of their school, I had to be patient and allow the staff to lead the conversation. They knew in their hearts that times and people had changed. There was a growing sense that the mission and vision needed to be revisited, but they were reluctant to revisit something in which they felt great ownership. My role simply became talking individually and collectively with teachers about where they were now, what they perceived to be the purpose of the school, and what the future might look like for them."

"Didn't that take a huge amount of time? That seems to be something I struggle with . . . trying to balance the external and management expectations with an appreciation of the humanness of the organization, honoring each person's needs." The troubled tone of Kari's question was evident.

Tom's deep sigh indicated his own appreciation for the difficulty of balancing the urgency of external demands with the knowledge that lasting, meaningful change requires people to be *responsible* for the change rather than just comply.

"It *did* take a lot of time, but it was well worth the discipline to move slowly. While we didn't make any decisions the first year, the topic of change was a theme in our conversations. In the second year, at the suggestion of the staff, we brought forward our thinking about mission and vision and couched it in terms of turning beliefs into actions. Over the course of the year, we refined our work into a publishable set of beliefs and the actions that supported those beliefs. At that point, it was easy to refer to them when making a decision or evaluating our work. Every person who walked through the door knew what we were about. It was an informal process, but explicit about what we would be doing."

Tom's recollection of what had transpired over the first year aligned with what he had voiced at the beginning of their conversation. Kari nodded in understanding and reflected upon what had taken place in her school, then began to share with Tom.

"I had already known many of the staff members because I had been a curriculum specialist, so I had some credibility with them. I knew many of the parents and students because I was involved in community programs. I lived near the school community. Still, this was a different role, so I needed to make sure I truly had a deep understanding of what this school stood for."

"It sounds as though you had a similar dilemma," Tom suggested, "but different conditions in which to work."

Kari thought for a moment about where to start. "As a part of modeling my leadership beliefs, I put together a description of what I was looking for in any staff member wanting to be more intimately involved in instructional and cultural leadership—those who would be in the forefront of reculturing the school. They would first connect with their colleagues, then be expected to come together to synthesize the hundreds of sheets of paper that identified people's deepest thoughts and wishes. These leaders would run many of the meetings, write the proceedings, and try to capture what people were feeling, while embracing and challenging as necessary when difficult issues or disagreements occurred."

"You know, Kari, some people might think of this as an 'elitist' position. Did you think about that? How did you plan to gauge how people felt about this structure?"

"The teachers were left to decide who would be a part of this group. I unquestioningly accepted and supported their decisions. It was amazing to see the commitment and resolve of this dedicated group of leaders and their impact on the rest of the staff and parents. This was borne out by the comments I heard and the observable results of their work. When people realized that I was simply a part of the process, they seemed to more readily express what was important to them. I enjoyed being on the sidelines, coaching and supporting, rather than directing. It was important for me to be visible and accessible, to demonstrate how much I valued each person through my actions and words. Remember our discussion about how empowering others leads to uncovering collective wisdom?"

When people realized that I was simply a part of the process, they seemed to more readily express what was important to them. I enjoyed being on the sidelines, coaching and supporting, rather than directing. It was important for me to be visible and accessible, to demonstrate how much I valued each person through my actions and words.

"Yes, I do," Tom affirmed, "and our collective wisdom allows us to see that effective leadership includes trust, shared leadership, and collaboration."

"One of the things I reminded people of when the drafts started coming in was that whatever we came up with would be the guiding principles of how we operated on a daily basis. We would be held accountable for our beliefs, and we would measure our actions against our beliefs. It was like running a marathon, complete with blisters, heaving chests, minds clouded with exhaustion, energy completely spent—but the sense of accomplishment radiated from all the tired, drawn faces. This was not a short, easy process. Everyone agreed that the hard work would provide the sustenance for all future endeavors."

"It sounds as though everyone put their hearts and souls into this process," Tom said admiringly. "For you, Kari, were there indicators that the hard work was changing the way people thought about themselves, how they saw each other, and how it was making a difference for children?"

"I believe so," she answered. "Here's one example. A staff member who had historically been reluctant to embrace the changes we were making came to me, shut the door of my office, took a piece of dark chocolate out of the basket on my desk, and asked if I had a minute. She immediately embarked upon a story about how a parent had just questioned a homework assignment she had sent home the previous week. In the past, she told me, she would have defended the assignment, knowing that she was the one with the degree in education. How dare the parent question what was decided by the expert! Rapidly, I began to consider how I was going to respond, as the actions she described did not match our written expectations about how we interact when concerns are brought forth. Something clicked, though, when I heard her say 'in the past.' I forced myself to listen to all she had to say. She went on to tell me that the work we had done to articulate what we stood for as a staff influenced the way she had responded to the situation. She realized that the parent was correct! Even though the standard for learning was stated and it was appropriate for the grade level, the directions were not clear, nor was there enough information about how the end product would demonstrate increased learning for the child. The teacher *knew* there were connections, since she had thoroughly planned the assignment. However, she just hadn't clearly explained how it all fit together to the parent, and probably to the student as well. Between the two of them—the parent and teacher talking together—they came up with an assignment that would make sense to both children and parents.

"The look on that teacher's face said it all," Kari concluded her story. "Relief, pride, and a strong sense of connectedness to our school were evident. Her reaction to this open conversation with the parent was a clear reflection of choosing to have her actions connect to and be supported by the beliefs that we, as a staff, had worked so hard and long to articulate."

"That must have provided you with a lot of satisfaction," Tom replied, "in judging the efficacy of your school's work."

"It certainly did." Kari stopped for a moment. "And I needed to be held accountable, too."

"Exposing our vulnerability as a leader is difficult at best and embarrassing at worst. Yet if we are going to walk our talk . . ." Tom's voice trailed off, and Kari picked up the thought.

Exposing our vulnerability as a leader is difficult at best and embarrassing at worst. Yet if we are going to walk our talk . . .

"Soon after we published and posted our mission, vision, and values, I was put to the test. When facilitating a Tuesday afternoon staff meeting, I noticed some quiet sidebar conversations and felt the inattentiveness of the group as a whole. It wasn't that people were being rude; they just weren't engaged, and I felt as though I was pulling teeth to get anyone to participate. I couldn't put my finger on what was happening. Finally, a voice rang out from the middle of the room. I saw Bob standing with a piece of paper in his hand. He asked respectfully but directly, 'Kari, how does the district mandate for this new literacy staff development apply to this document?' He held aloft the copy of our mission, vision, and values. The room grew silent. Time seemed to stand still as all eyes focused on me. On one hand, I was excited that people were holding me accountable and referring to our collective work, yet I also realized that I didn't know the answer. I hadn't been fully informed by the district and didn't know the entire purpose of the training."

"Ouch," Tom winced. "So leadership is rooted in our humanity, not in a checklist of things to do. Back to *being* a leader rather than *doing* leadership."

"Right on target, Tom. I also realized that effective leaders don't always know the answer, and it's critical to admit and embrace that we need to dig deeper and rely on others, because we can sometimes become trapped and unable to hear and fully consider the views of others. I quickly realized this was the moment that would determine whether or not the environment was conducive to risk taking without penalty, to trust that ideas would be honored and that people would be treated with respect. With this in mind, I encouraged the staff to discuss their concern, and I stepped back both physically and verbally. They could now discuss the 'undiscussables,' but they needed to see that I would not sabotage their conversations. Bob's question was posed in a way that indicated there was beginning to be a fundamental shift in how we operated. It was not a personal attack, but rather a commitment to do whatever it would take to fulfill our guiding principles. After the discussion ended, I let Bob know that I appreciated his willingness to question in a respectful manner that held us to our focus on student success. That staff meeting set the conditions under which we continue to operate today."

Effective leaders don't always know the answer, and it's critical to admit and embrace that we need to dig deeper and rely on others, because we can sometimes become trapped and unable to hear and fully consider the views of others.

"It's tremendously exciting when we see the manifestations of our work," Tom added. Both Tom and Kari paused, taking in the significance of their conversation. "Where are those notes you started to take?" Tom asked.

Kari dug them out from under the pile of books and papers they had brought. She had thought they would glean great insight from the theoretical texts. Interestingly enough, however, the texts had provided inspiration for what could be, not a recipe for how to be effective leaders. She handed the notepad to Tom, who pulled out his pen and added to the list of qualities they were compiling.

Communicate	Clarify
Identify purpose	Align mission/vision/values
Be visible	Provide consistent monitoring
"Be with us" mentality	Hold expectations (behavior and learning)

After looking at what had been jotted down so far, both principals realized that while culture is important—constantly in flux and always needing to be attended to—they couldn't forget that leaders must also be learners.

Kari began, "When we ask teachers to take a class in order to increase their expertise in the curriculum and effective practices, we need to take it with them. When we ask teachers to implement their learning, we ask them to do it together, collaboratively, providing feedback to each other about what worked or didn't work. When we discover that lots of students are experiencing the 'ah-ha's' and the teaching is resulting in learning, we celebrate together. When we notice that some are still struggling, we collectively determine exactly what is keeping the child from being successful, plan, and follow through. Our sole focus is to be open to every possibility we can create in support of every child."

"Your passion for every child and every adult's success is evident, but you don't simply just *wish* it to be so," Tom said. "It seems to me that you cast yourself in the role of lead learner." He continued, sharing his reflections from the conversation. "You model the importance of paying attention to the needs of the people in the school organization to enable them to do their very best work on behalf of the children. I heard you talk about understanding what you need to learn, bringing people together and lifting their hearts. I heard the importance of taking the time to celebrate and recognizing the positive actions happening in your school. And what I understand, Kari, is that all of this conversation about school leadership—empowering, trusting, respecting, being clear about expectations and purpose—centers on the effective implementation of curriculum, and student learning."

"Testing and assessment is absolutely part of our reality. We *should* be held accountable," Kari built on what Tom had said. "How else can we determine that we're continuing to refine our teaching and hold high expectations for every child? However, I know that it makes a huge impact on people when they are recognized. The smallest recognition can be just as significant as a big award. I recently had a phone message from a parent, thanking me for sending a postcard to her child. I wrote that I had seen her child realize that his teammate across the table was struggling with addition and was beginning to show frustration by breaking his pencil. So I wrote to him that I appreciated his willingness to reach out and help his friend. The two kids' heads truly were operating as one; the task was completed without the teacher even having to intervene."

"Sounds like noticing something small and sharing it with one person created recognition for many. The child knows that he was noticed by you, and indirectly you recognized the parent. In the end, you received recognition right back!"

Adults also need to know that they are going to be noticed for what important things they do to support each other and the children at our school.

"You're right again, Tom! That makes me remember that adults also need to know that they are going to be noticed for what important things they do to support each other and the children at our school. I started out writing quick notes to staff—just a couple of lines about something I observed during the day. Many times it was as simple as, 'Thanks for taking the time to review the day's math lesson with your new teammate.' Or, 'After you spent two minutes calming Johnny down from a recess incident, he went into class with his tears dried and focused on his work.' Staff members are now writing notes to each other, seeing the incredible impact that occurs when we make the choice to lift spirits rather than diminish them. Comments on report cards and weekly folders are more about direct observation and less about teacher judgment. They are more apt to provide a suggestion that honors or recognizes where a child is and what he can do, and ask for support from the parent in order to ensure success."

Kari leaned back, feeling a sense of pride about what had transpired in her school, while Tom wrote the following:

Learn together	Learn individually
Teach effectively	Identify learning goals
Praise	Recognize
Look for positives	Give specific feedback
Connect learning and feedback to mission/vision/values/goals	

Kari's cell phone began to ring, interrupting the pause in their joint reflections. She picked up her phone and turned off the ring, apologizing for the inconvenience. Then she gasped in amazement when she saw the time on the phone display.

"Do you realize that we have been talking for over three hours?"

"You're kidding!" Tom looked up with surprise. "I feel as though we've just scratched the surface of what it means to be an effective leader. This conversation has been so engaging and meaningful for me! It just proves that when people are engaged in something they love, it doesn't feel like work. What I really liked about this was the back-and-forth nature of the conversation, how you not only listened to me, but asked questions that encouraged me to go deeper with my own thinking."

"There are so many more lessons we can learn from each other," Kari exulted. "I've already gleaned lots of ideas from you! If we create these same kinds of opportunities for teachers, wouldn't we be promoting rich learning and increased expertise, which in turn would lead to increased student learning?"

"You know, Kari, part of being an effective leader is knowing that leadership exists in *everyone*. Our job is to do what we can to uncover it and bring it to light, then encourage it to spread to others."

Kari nodded in agreement while Tom showed her the notepad with the list of key words they had generated during their time together. Silently, they considered what was written, and both were incredulous that this conversation not only reinforced what they knew, but it also was infused with new perspectives and an appreciation for *being* a leader, not *doing* leadership.

Tom thought for a moment, then said, "Being a leader is working and acting so as to empower others to do their most creative and effective work in a way that supports the common mission, vision, and values of the organization. A key to this is *trust*—trust in people's commitment to the shared purpose, trust in their willingness and skill in collaborative endeavors, trust in their personal and collective wisdom, and a trust that they are able to open their hearts and minds to each other in order to face the obstacles and challenges that will occur."

Kari agreed with Tom's conviction that having the courage to trust others enables a leader to recognize and access the best in everyone, including oneself.

"Just checking things off of a lengthy 'To-Do List' is not enough, because it doesn't transcend to others. While it is a part of leadership, the piece that is missing is that it doesn't empower others to move toward developing their own leadership capacity," Kari added.

Kari and Tom both recognized, after a lot of thoughtful conversation, that even though there are many challenges in *being* a leader, at the heart lies unending possibilities to illuminate the leadership in others. And with that in mind, and the coffee cups drained, they headed back out into the December morning.

Thomas J. Kasper and Kari Cocozzella are practicing elementary principals in two large suburban districts located in the Denver metropolitan area. When invited to share everyday stories about their experiences as educational leaders, they quickly found common ground in the belief that leadership resides at all levels in a school community. Even though they had never shared an extended conversation prior to this collaboration, they soon realized that both held an unyielding commitment to encouraging leadership, developing leadership capacity, and accepting leadership from others in order to create the conditions in a school which afford every student and adult the opportunity to access and engage in learning for life.

CHAPTER SIX

OUT-OF-THE-BOX LEADERSHIP

A Reflection on Leading Educational Transformation

JANE A. KENDRICK

T his chapter contains some of my personal reflections on "out-of-the-box leadership." It is based on my experiences during the time I spent as principal of an urban middle school, as superintendent of a PreK–12 urban school district, and as a consultant for strategic professional development to a large-city school district. For purposes of this chapter, I am describing out-of-the-box leadership as both thinking and action that result in improved and sustained transformation of educational practices, leading to increased performance of staff and students.

Incidentally, promoting and engaging in out-of-the-box leadership should in no way negate the importance and purpose of continuing to engage in some *in*-the-box leadership—which is important in attending to the necessary, structured work of education and in maintaining important traditions and improving required practices. A key understanding for leaders today is knowing when and how to lead both in the box and outside the box—often simultaneously.

A prerequisite to leading outside the box is *thinking* outside the box. This requires a set of attributes including, but not limited to, being open to different ideas and solutions, listening to others, and supporting others when they come up with new ideas. Leading outside the box requires a variety of skills, but for the purposes of my reflection, I shall limit my discussion to the one skill that I deem most important in leading transformational change: building personal capacity and building the capacity of the systems we lead.

In the following paragraphs, I describe some of my actual experiences in my journey of attempting to create transformational change by building capacity in my roles of principal and superintendent. I am also developing a "personal road map" to guide my own work in my latest educational leadership challenge—leading transformational change of high schools in a large-city school district. In each case, my comments are organized specifically around the leadership attributes of out-of-the-box leadership, as described above.

BUILDING PERSONAL LEADERSHIP CAPACITY

One particular professional development experience in my career has greatly influenced my ability to think "out of the box." That experience was participating as a facilitator in the Indiana Principals Leadership Academy (IPLA). I was fortunate to have been selected to participate in this program, as it focused not on "what was," but rather on what "could be" if school leaders thought about their work and roles as leaders with new vision and new understandings. IPLA focused on developing leadership skills that went beyond traditional training, focusing on harnessing individual and group creativity and developing participatory facilitation skills.

Indiana Principals Leadership Academy (IPLA)

In 1985, the Indiana General Assembly passed House Enrolled Act 1236, which called for the establishment of the Indiana Principals Leadership Academy. In the initial discussions, it was agreed that a principals academy should be a unique, innovative approach to professional development.

To develop the concept, a think tank of more than 70 people met during the summer of 1986. The think tank consisted of elementary, middle school, and high school educators; university and college representatives; business leaders; superintendents; and parents. The

Promoting and engaging in out-of-the-box leadership should in no way negate the importance and purpose of continuing to engage in some in-the-box leadership.

challenge was to create a vision for the IPLA. (A vision is a statement of the very best that one can imagine, stated as if it already existed.) So, from its onset, IPLA focused on out-of-the-box thinking, especially in terms of its focus on risk taking and looking beyond the obvious for solutions and opportunities. The following quote, which can be found on the IPLA Web site,[1] captures, through its analogy, the ongoing focus and out-of-the-box framework of IPLA:

In taking a close look at the giraffe, there didn't seem to be a more fitting symbol for the Academy. We learned that the average adult giraffe weighs about 2,000 pounds, making it a giant of an animal. Amazingly, the average giraffe heart weighs approximately 25 pounds. Because of their height, the giraffe has a couple of advantages. First of all they are able to reach the leaves at the top of the trees. These leaves are the freshest and closest to the sun. Secondly, they are able to see far into the distance, truly making them an animal with vision. At the same time what gives them advantages can also lead to risks. To reach the leaves at the top of the trees, the giraffe must stabilize its body by slightly spreading its legs. It is at this point that the giraffe is most vulnerable to its predator. To get the very best, to be the very best, the giraffe must stick its neck out and take a risk. And so we thought the same applied to us. If we are to be the best we must be willing to stick our necks out and take risks . . . especially for kids.

In the fall of 1986, a total of 15 peer facilitators were selected from across the state to develop the curriculum and program components for IPLA. I was one of the fortunate ones selected to participate in this unique and groundbreaking opportunity, primarily because I had been trained in the School Improvement Process (SIP) and was having some success with school improvement as a principal. The IPLA training included being informed about futures forecasting and investigating successful leadership models from the best practices of leaders throughout the world. Thinking and leading out of the box were major criteria as we began the process of designing the IPLA curriculum and dissemination model.

We began our program development by reviewing what the think tank had developed in terms of program and process. The focus of the academy was not to be on management, but rather on the development of facilitation skills that would lead to "significant" school improvement. A key element of the program included viewing the role of the principal differently than traditional higher education principal programs—focusing on the role of principal as facilitator of change, rather than just a manager of the three B's—*b*udgets, *b*uses, and *b*utts.

The key belief undergirding all activities of the academy was that real improvement in schools could not occur until the majority of stakeholders had "voice," i.e., they were involved in key decisions that affected their work and were given the opportunity to discuss improvement strategies before those strategies were imposed on them from "on high." In essence, the belief was that everyone affected by a decision should have some input into that decision.

After careful study and mentoring from our program director, Gerald DeWitt, our group of peer facilitators identified the following topics and processes for Year 1 of the academy. Facilitation processes included brainstorming, vision building, consensus building, and team building. The curriculum content focused on adult learning styles, leadership strengths and deployment, demographic trends, and time-management strategies.

Ideally, brainstorming should be nonthreatening, but I still recall the panic of many of our first-year participants as they were encouraged to think "out of the box" and let their imaginations run free. Given the time frame of the inaugural year of IPLA (1986), and the socio-demographic realities of the principalship in Indiana at that time, the vast majority of our participants were white males. Many were pragmatic, no-nonsense types; they had what seemed to be an innate distrust of any process that appeared to be "touchy-feely" and did not immediately produce results. We were inundated with complaints about the use of such a "time-wasting" process. A persistent lament was, "Why do we have to list anything that comes to mind when we know half of it is unrealistic?" After a couple of sessions, the participants actually started referring to brainstorming as the "B" word! The good news was that we had most of the participants for a two-year stint, so by the beginning of Year 2, most had become experts themselves at leading these sessions. Later, the value of brainstorming became increasingly clear as we led participants through the vision-building process.

Creating vision in the absence of true brainstorming will often lead to in-the-box thinking, which may or may not be satisfactory in leading a school to the place it "ought to be." Regurgitating old problems without different thinking will result in the same old solutions. In IPLA, participants were taught to define vision as "the place where we see ourselves down the road." Vision statements were to be out of the box, futuristic, and expressed in the present tense. Statements of vision were also to include a glimpse of the state of academic, social, and personal efficacy of the students and adults in the school.

Creating vision in the absence of true brainstorming will often lead to in-the-box thinking, which may or may not be satisfactory in leading a school to the place it "ought to be."

Vision statements were created using a consensus-building process. Consensus was defined as the agreement that an overwhelming majority of stakeholders could live with the decision and would not block progress toward its implementation. In this process, we were guided in learning strategies that would ensure that all voices were heard in the process, that all responses were clarified for accuracy, that all responses were condensed as much as possible without distorting meaning, and that all responses were grouped into theme areas and prioritized in terms of their importance. This process of vision building through consensus requires all involved to share their thoughts and opinions and to move beyond "voting" for impact in the final decision.

Embedded in the vision- and consensus-building process was team building. Out-of-the-box leadership recognizes and seeks voices other than one's own to develop and implement strategies for success and improvement. The team-building activities used in the IPLA curriculum were ongoing—a part of every session. This process also required leaders to behave out of the box, as well as take risks. Many of the activities required role playing, group activities, and using right-brain activities.

Although there were other, more traditional aspects to the IPLA training, without doubt the strategies I have described above required participants to get out of their comfort zones and participate in (if not embrace) out-of-the-box thinking. It educated us about the power of vision to move organization versus stand-alone goal setting, the importance of teams versus the convenience of solo decision making, and the impact of consensus decision making versus voting. With the passage of P.L. 221 in Indiana in 1998 came the requirement that all schools have some sort of shared decision-making council. I am confident that the leaders who went through IPLA in its early years were well prepared to lead in an era that values and requires shared decision making.

BUILDING BUILDING-LEVEL CAPACITY

Although several professional development experiences during my career provided training in leading change as a school leader, only one of them was really a comprehensive process aimed at building the capacity to support and sustain change. That experience was the /I/D/E/A/ School Improvement Process (SIP).

My tenure as principal of Henry W. Eggers Middle School in Hammond, Indiana, began in the fall of 1978 and continued through the spring of 1991. As determined by the Iowa Tests of Basic Skills in 1977, the majority of our eighth graders were testing at two grade levels below expectations in vocabulary, reading comprehension, math computation, math concepts, and math application. Out-of-school suspensions were the highest in the district, and the percentage of African American students suspended was double that of enrollment percentages.

Eggers Middle School, though only four years old in 1978, was already suffering from a shaky reputation brought on by low achievement and the perception that the school's discipline was out of control. For the first several years, I concentrated on transactional leadership practices, working clearly within the "box" to shore up a shaky culture and unacceptable practices, both among the faculty and the student body. My primary leadership style was to do those things that would result in more "law and order" so that learning could occur. I spent a lot of time regulating, delegating, and dictating procedures, practices, and standards. Only after I was certain that the culture was ready did

I begin to explore building capacity among the faculty and community to support and sustain school improvement.

I was also fortunate that the school district of Hammond had already invested the time and resources to structure the Eggers staff into teaching teams. The school had introduced the interdisciplinary, or "learning community," concept three years prior to my arrival—specifically to make the organization more responsive to the needs of students and more congruent with the physical structure, which was an "open concept"

Only after I was certain that the culture was ready did I begin to explore building capacity among the faculty and community to support and sustain school improvement.

school. In a document describing this Learning Community Project, the following statements were listed as the purposes of the project:

1. To establish a team of teachers who can plan together the academic program of their students

2. To permit teachers to know their students better socially and academically

3. To design a structure in which there is the flexibility to plan academic programs with individual differences in mind

4. To call an academic planning time together on a regular basis

5. To have teachers in a better position to communicate with parents about student academic and behavioral progress

6. To permit teachers to plan use of time and space according to the needs of their learning community of 140 students

Learning communities were a spin-off of the IGE (Individually Guided Education) model and were a grandparent of Professional Learning Communities (PLCs). From 1978 through 1983, I focused on building the capacity of our learning communities by developing new roles and rules for the operation of the interdisciplinary teams. Regular meetings between the team leaders were scheduled and conducted by the administration, and team leaders were held accountable for the progress of their team's work as reported weekly to me.

As a direct consequence of this intervention, discipline problems throughout the school diminished, as did out-of-school suspensions. The climate of the school continued to improve, and the stage was set to dramatically tackle student achievement. It was at this time in our journey that we were offered an opportunity to participate in a systematic process to take us to the next level of capacity building in terms of developing systemwide leadership and knowledge about best instructional practices and improvement strategies.

/I/D/E/A/ School Improvement Process (SIP)

Building capacity in the faculty of a school requires risk taking and rethinking (out of the box) existing rules, roles, and relationships. It requires leaders who are willing to share their weaknesses and model being lifelong learners. Frankly, I found that these were skills and talents for which I was ill prepared. Fortunately, our journey into site-based management in Hammond began at the forefront of the national movement and immediately prior to the release of the momentous "A Nation at Risk" report. I volunteered to participate in SIP training in the earliest stages of its implementation in Hammond. This early involvement is the primary reason I was able to learn to systematically engage in leadership out of the box.

"A Nation at Risk" in 1983 underscored the urgent need for out-of-the-box leadership in U.S. schools. With the release of this report came many recommendations, including the benefits of driving key decisions close to the point of impact and implementation—often at the school and classroom levels.

Building capacity in the faculty of a school requires risk taking and rethinking (out of the box) existing rules, roles, and relationships.

During this period, many school districts adopted versions of site-based management, school councils, and other decentralized decision-making processes. The implied goal of these changes was simple: If we keep on doing what we've always done, we'll get what we always got—and that was not good enough to keep the United States competitive. Many principals, teachers, and superintendents across the nation ventured out of their known and traditional boxes of leadership thinking to experiment with different versions of site-based management, with the express purpose of improving teaching and learning. I was one of them.

In so doing, we were asked to embrace notions and ideas that were often foreign to our formal schooling tenets and past practices. The adjectives most often used during those times to describe great school principals were "risk takers" and "entrepreneurs." Some out-of-the-box state and local educational leaders encouraged principals to go beyond their traditional thinking to forge new relationships with teachers, parents, and the community. The strengths of the decentralization movement that I observed encompassed increased teacher and parent involvement in key school decisions, including scheduling, curriculum, and public relations; serious attention to issues of school climate, particularly as they related to student discipline, attendance, and achievement; a renewed focus on professional development; enhanced teacher efficacy; and, most significantly, increased student achievement.

The concept of improvement, as represented in the /I/D/E/A/ (1979) guidelines, is referred to as SIP (School Improvement Process).[2] SIP stresses two fundamental characteristics: First, improvement is not described as a series of discrete steps or as a system of broad leaps, but rather as a representation of continuous improvement. Second, each stage subsumes all previous levels in a kind of "all before and more" system, characterized by the ongoing involvement of several groups of individuals. The SIP model, as a strategic planning process, is appropriate for schools with varying degrees of organizational health. And, depending on the nature of the individual school situation, embracing the plan may or may not be a major risk and threat to the administration.

SIP begins with a vision: the visualization and thinking—out of the box—of the "best we can imagine for our school." Improvement as depicted through the process deals not only with program improvement, but also with ownership of decisions, program implementation, and governance. The purpose of SIP is to create an organizational culture that perceives decision making as a shared responsibility and opportunity. Given the realities of schools in the early 1980s (typically cultures that were indoctrinated and immersed in top-down decision making), the venture into shared governance was in itself a big risk and represented genuine out-of-the-box leadership.

SIP is a training and implementation process that builds the capacity of the building-level staff to design and implement strategies of school improvement and transformational change. The following components characterize 12 steps to an improved organizational culture. The SIP process was developed by the Institute for the Development of Educational Activities (/I/D/E/A/), which had its headquarters in Dayton, Ohio.[3]

Vision of Excellence: The improvement team develops a clear picture of where the school is headed and what the organization will be like when the participants have attained their vision, or "the best they can imagine."

Ownership and Governance: Anyone affected by a decision is involved in making it. The organization is designed so that all participants are encouraged to influence key decisions that affect their professional destiny.

Formative Evaluation: Decisions are made based on data, not on hearsay or instinct. Systematic efforts are made to "keep score" by collecting data, which insures success by "correcting in flight."

Celebrating Excellence: The pursuit of excellence is rewarded within the school. Personal and professional improvement is acknowledged and valued both by the teaching staff and the administration. Improvement is made attractive by specific organizational supports of all participants.

Focus Forecast Group: Professional staff work in teams to solve problems, to improve programs, and to increase job satisfaction. Peer assistance is a common source of professional improvement with time, resources, and access to new information provided for this activity. Such groups assume four roles: keeper of the vision, formative evaluator, decision maker, and problem solver.

Public Relations: The power of the "grapevine," or informal networks, is used to inform parents and community about program improvement. A pyramiding mechanism exists for keeping the school community informed and involved.

Staff Development: A long-range, comprehensive program keeps professional staff current on the latest research and practices. Skill-building sessions that use methods compatible with "how adults learn" are provided regularly.

Instructional Leadership: Someone is clearly responsible for providing leadership for instructional improvement. Instructional supervision and assistance are provided for all staff, and expectations for improvement are modeled by "champions." The champions, or leaders, must be willing to take risks and lead out of the box.

Personal/Professional Plans for Improvement: There is an expectation of improvement both on a personal and program level. Personal/professional goal setting is practiced by staff and modeled by leaders.

Resource Support: Time, materials, and information are provided for professional and program improvement efforts. The organization supports action research and field testing of new ideas through mini-grants, released time, and continuous access to new research and out-of-the-box practices.

New Roles; New Participants: Home and community are recognized as educating institutions. Business partnerships with schools assist in the education of youth. Parents are informed and within the home assume responsible roles that complement the efforts of the school. Students are expected to contribute to school improvement through planned programs.

Timeline, Design, Implementation: While the organization is primarily proactive with future forecasts and plans of prevention, there are procedures that use the best ideas and resources of the school to generate hopeful solutions and corrective plans of action for emerging problems. Long-range implementation strategies with assigned tasks and timelines are kept vivid to participants.

"Out-of-the-box leadership and thinking" is a fundamental component of SIP, since the entire process begins with the creation of a vision. As a culmination of the first few meetings, the SIP planning team creates a vision of "the best we can imagine for our school." This vision is generated through brainstorming and is narrowed down and finally precisely articulated through consensus-building activities. The vision statement does not enumerate specific activities or outcomes, but it does indicate out-of-the-box thinking. It represents a desirable or, at times, an unattainable state. The vision statement is accompanied by a set of goals, each focusing on specific outcomes.

The first vision for Eggers Middle School stated a lofty and aggressive goal—particularly so when one takes into consideration the state of the school at the time of SIP implementation. During that period, students at Eggers were performing well below expectations. The following vision statement, created by the SIP process, went way out of the box, both in terms of its reach and its aggressiveness:

The vision statement does not enumerate specific activities or outcomes, but it does indicate out-of-the-box thinking. It represents a desirable or, at times, an unattainable state.

> The community of Eggers School is committed to excellence in education. Our priorities during the next five years will assure that our school is recognized as one of the best in the country.

The goals established by the SIP team were also lofty, but seemingly more attainable:

> One hundred percent involvement of staff, students, and parents in the educational program as evidenced by instructional practices, student achievement, conduct, and attendance.
>
> Enthusiasm and commitment to processes of instruction that will lead to attainment of mastery by all students.
>
> Consistency of behavioral and academic standards within teaching teams and among teaching teams.
>
> Commitment to processes identified to diagnose and prescribe to various learning styles.
>
> Consistent and conscientious follow-through with academic prescriptions for various learning styles, learning strengths, and learning weaknesses.

From the onset of our initial training in SIP in 1983, and continuing beyond my tenure at Eggers, which ended in 1991, there was ongoing involvement with school improvement. Although there were many highlights of our progress during this decade, perhaps the most significant in terms of the vision and goals was the recognition received by the school in 1988 as one of the nation's Blue Ribbon Secondary Schools. So, by one national standard, Eggers did indeed attain its vision of "being recognized as one of the best secondary schools in the country."

The school improvement process is not an easy one to implement; it requires consistent and involved leadership. It must become the modus operandi of the organization and second nature to key stakeholders of the school. If it is viewed merely as a series of meetings rather than a process, it will be as ineffective as other in-the-box processes that get occasional attention with routine results. SIP is much more than a planning process; it is a systemic and organic way of functioning—establishing a vision and working diligently and thoughtfully toward that overarching destination.

BUILDING SCHOOL DISTRICT CAPACITY

Although I have participated in many assessment and accreditation processes over the course of my career, only one professional development experience has enabled me to thoughtfully and systematically engage in leading systemic transformation at the district level. That experience was the Standard-Bearer School District process (SBSD) developed by Phillip C. Schlechty and his associates at the Schlechty Center for Leadership in School Reform.

In 1988, Schlechty launched the Center for Leadership in School Reform as a means of providing high-quality, responsive support to those who are leading school reform efforts across the nation. A private, nonprofit corporation with headquarters in Louisville, Kentucky, the Schlechty Center works with public school districts and their leaders to transform the existing system of rules, roles, and relationships that govern the way resources are used in schools into a system that is focused on the quality of work provided to students.

The SBSD process incorporates 10 district standards, grouped around the development of three system capacities:

- The Capacity to Focus on the Future (shared understanding of the need for change, shared beliefs, and vision)
- The Capacity to Maintain Direction and Focus (focus on the student and product quality, participatory leadership, results-oriented decision making, and continuity)

- The Capacity for Strategic Action (support, innovation and flexibility, technology, and collaboration)[4]

During my career as principal, I was often discouraged and angered by the seemingly destructive and arbitrary decision making passed down from the central office. Given that Hammond was a groundbreaking district using site-based management, and given that both the superintendent of schools and the leader of the local teacher union were recognized forerunners in this regard, it was even more perplexing and troublesome that our progress at the building level was sometimes thwarted.

It was during this time that I met Phil Schlechty and began discussions about the importance of the entire system in the support of transformational change at the building level. During my conversations with Schlechty, I realized that the issues we faced were not the result of the attitudes of key leaders; they were a direct result of the system that was in place—a system focused on regulating rather than on building capacity. The standard-bearer framework provides a means to unify ongoing initiatives and bring coherence to district efforts—where the core business is, or should be, providing students with content-rich, engaging work every day.

During my career as principal, I was often discouraged and angered by the seemingly destructive and arbitrary decision making passed down from the central office.

My superintendency in Anderson, Indiana, began in the spring of 1993. One of the major challenges I faced was improving the relationships between the district and the teacher union. The recent history of labor relations in the district had been steeped in conflict; the climate could best be described as "testy." I brought with me an attitude that we would all work together to create a vision and a new operating style that was based on inclusion and consensus. Although most of the secondary schools and several elementary schools were already engaged in site-based management, I knew we needed to tackle systemic issues if the climate for change and the rules and structures to support change were to be dramatically altered at the district level. I invited Schlechty to work with us to help us redefine our roles, relationships, and rules around systemic transformation.

We began by working through the standards of what would later be called the SBSD process.

System Capacity I: The Ability to Focus on the Future

The first capacity of SBSD focuses on vision and belief. In other words, did key leaders of the district—including the superintendent, school board trustees, union leaders, and community leaders—have a shared understanding of the need for change? And if they did have that shared understanding, did they agree on what needed to be changed and how it needed to be changed? The answer to all of those questions was no. There was no shared understanding, nor were there shared beliefs about what should happen to improve the quality of education.

For example, some members of the school board believed that the major problem regarding the quality of education was teacher attitudes and resistance to change. Union leaders thought the major problem hindering improvement was the attitudes of parents and students. Some community leaders thought the major problems facing the district were created as a direct result of a teacher union that had been spoiled over the years and not held accountable for results. Clearly, there was much work to be done to develop consensus.

We began the dialogue by having Schlechty present reasons why the schools of today are woefully inadequate in terms of preparing students for the twenty-first century, and how rules, roles, and relationships in the system need to be dramatically altered to ensure that more students learn at higher levels. In a series of lectures shared with the key stakeholder groups, he presented the reasons for change and for creating district capacity to support that change.

During this initial awareness phase, most participants heard the message that the primary workers in schools should be the students, and that teachers should focus on creating engaging knowledge work. To that end, schools should focus on the things they did have control over, such as the qualities of schoolwork. They should spend less time focusing on things they could not control, such as the lack of involvement and support from some parents. This message was accepted by many, but rejected by others who adhered to their belief that if kids would just "do what they were told" and respect teachers, and if parents would just support the schools as they once did, things would improve and teachers could teach.

——————— ⚜ ———————

Schools should focus on the things they did have control over, such as the qualities of schoolwork. They should spend less time focusing on things they could not control, such as the lack of involvement and support from some parents.

After several attempts to disseminate the message about why education needed dramatic transformation, our next step was to create a systemic approach to having frequent and ongoing engagement in our efforts to develop a set of beliefs and values about education that key stakeholders in the district could support. To facilitate this dialogue, I formed a professional learning community called Kaleidoscope. The Kaleidoscope community included officers of the teacher union, myself, the assistant superintendents, three board members, two community members, and three principals. We met each month to discuss (and cuss about) our differences in efforts to reach consensus on our beliefs about students' abilities to learn, our roles in enabling them to learn, and the roles of others in the district in creating the capacity for students to learn.

The Kaleidoscope community met many times over the course of several months to develop a vision that was based on shared beliefs and values. Our work finally culminated in the development of the ACS (Anderson Community Schools) Constitution, which would serve as the road map and guide for future actions and decision making on behalf of the district. The constitution still appears on the Anderson Community Schools Web site, 10 years after its development.[5]

System Capacity II: Maintaining Direction and Focus

Upon finalizing the constitution, we formed several learning communities at both the school and district levels to discuss student work. We reviewed the qualities of schoolwork as defined by Schlechty's Working on the Work (WOW) framework.[6] In addition to addressing the qualities of student work, we also engaged in significant levels of professional development to provide our principals and teacher leaders with the skills necessary to assess the quality of their assignments. We began to systematically engage in reviewing student work and making those discussions part of our culture. The language we used to discuss student work was changing in positive ways.

Along with the emphasis on student work and the design qualities of that work, we continued to work toward a system of participatory leadership throughout the district. Much to the chagrin of some of my executive team, I invited the president of the local union to join our weekly cabinet meetings. I believed then, as I do now, that there is more to be gained than lost from this type of open communication.

This was out-of-the-box thinking, in that my goal was to minimize errors in secondhand communication between the district's executive team and the union leadership. It minimized the necessity of bringing the union into the loop and served to enhance trust between union and management.

Unfortunately, these efforts were not long-lasting, nor did they become a systemic practice. My successor had a different set of marching orders from his school board, and being "cozy" with the union was not among them. So, despite several years of attempting to create conditions that fostered real trust and collaboration, the beliefs that undergirded this practice were not carried over to the next administration. There continued to be much discussion about the roles of building-based improvement teams in a district that had embraced site-based management prior to my administration. It seemed to be acceptable for buildings to be run by the principles of shared decision making, but that never became the case at the district level during my eight-year tenure.

Perhaps one of the most difficult challenges facing leaders is creating the capacity to manage by results. Even more challenging in school districts is working with the revolving-door system—not only of superintendents but also of school board trustees. To manage well by results, one must have a clear road map, stated benchmarks, and constancy of purpose. With every new board member comes a new agenda, unless the

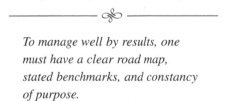

To manage well by results, one must have a clear road map, stated benchmarks, and constancy of purpose.

current board maintains a majority and continues to educate itself and its new members about the vision, beliefs, values, and priorities of the district.

Although we created a strategic plan and reported regularly on the progress of that plan, the process of managing by results never got "bone deep" during my tenure. The forces that often compel a school district to stray from its targets were well in play in Anderson. Those forces included a budget deficit that could only be corrected by additional revenues or dramatic downsizing. So, instead of focusing on results in our efforts to create capacity in the district, we were derailed early in our work with the daunting task of closing a high school, which created dissension, fear, and resistance throughout the district and community.

Unless a district has the capacity to maintain its focus on the results of its capacity-building process, it has little hope of maintaining the level of continuity required to persist in its vision and action strategies. When districts hit bumps in the road, they tend to derail rather than self-correct. Vision is often put on the back burner as the sense of urgency tends to become focused on the issue, or disruption, at hand. It is very difficult to lead with vision during turbulent times, but that is exactly what the SBSD process can provide if it has the time to become institutionalized in the policies and culture of the district.

When the Anderson board, after many months of discussion, finally decided to close a high school, the backlash was so serious that it caused many of us to retreat and spend the majority of our time putting out fires instead of focusing on the standard-bearer transformation. Although we attempted to continue with the SBSD process, and still focused on the vision and the quality of student work, it became increasingly more difficult to make that our priority.

In the first board election following the closing of a high school and the transition from three to two high schools, three of the incumbent board members decided not to run for reelection, sensing that they would be defeated as part of a backlash to their decision to consolidate. These three members had been very active in the development of the constitution and in the activities of Kaleidoscope. Without their membership on the board, it was necessary to go back and revisit the vision and beliefs. Unfortunately, I did not insist on taking the time to circle back to the vision and constitution, which would have educated the new members and reminded the rest of us of the importance of our transformation and capacity building.

System Capacity III: Strategic Action

Creating the capacity to support innovation, risk taking, and opportunity making may be inherent in some people, but it is not inherent in school systems. School systems are designed to enforce compliance, and Anderson was no exception to that rule. There was ongoing debate regarding the parameters of building teams in decision making, including the out-of-the-box thinking of some staff members who had created unique, break-the-mold programs for students. There was no avenue built into the system to systematically review and support invention. Therefore, it was left up to the school leaders and the superintendent to support risk taking that was often considered to be a threat to existing policy, particularly the collective bargaining agreement.

During my tenure, we were able to launch two out-of-the-box initiatives that supported innovation and flexibility through the use of technology. I have long been a proponent of technology interventions, particularly ones that can level the playing field for some of our students who are deprived of key support systems. One of those strategies was in response to a national grant sponsored by the U.S. Department of Education to create technology systems that could bridge the achievement gap between students of various socioeconomic backgrounds.

Our initiative, which was funded, was called the ACT NOW! Buddy Project; it resulted in computers being placed in the homes of all of our fourth-grade students. Although there were many mistakes made in the implementation of this project (and, I hope, many lessons learned from this experience), the district was at least willing to risk thinking beyond traditional approaches to ensure equity of opportunity for its students. What we did not prepare to do well was follow some of the lessons we were learning through site-based decision making and create the capacity to support the implementation of such an out-of-the-box approach. The other launch was the development of an alternative high school in a nontraditional school setting, the Options Program at Mounds Mall.

Creating the capacity to support innovation, risk taking, and opportunity making may be inherent in some people, but it is not inherent in school systems. School systems are designed to enforce compliance.

The culmination of a two-year partnership with the community was the development of the Technoplaza Learning Environment.[7] I had first learned of the Technoplaza when, with the other members of Kaleidoscope, I attended the first of the Arthur Andersen Futures

Meetings. At the time, leadership of the consulting division of the Andersen Corporation (now referred to as Accenture) were sponsoring conferences for school leaders focusing on out-of-the-box ideas as well as cutting-edge and promising initiatives. One initiative that grabbed our attention was an interactive learning environment using technology, team teaching, and facilitative teaching. The Technoplaza approach supports differentiated instruction, using teachers as coaches or guides, and provides opportunities for students to demonstrate learning using a wide variety of technology, including media.

Our work in the Anderson Community Schools was cut short by pressing issues that had little or nothing to do with improving instruction or developing the capacity of the district to support and sustain instructional improvement. We were sidetracked by the real, messy issues of school district management, including downsizing and seeking additional revenue both in terms of the general budget and for building improvements. We had not made it far enough along in our SBSD process to ensure continuity and sustainable results. I left the district in 2001, having exhausted my will to continue the struggle.

My Latest Journey in Out-of-the-Box Leadership

I have recently accepted a role directing the transformation of small high schools in Indianapolis. This improvement initiative is being paid for in part by a grant from the Bill and Melinda Gates Foundation through the Center for Leadership in Learning (CELL) at the University of Indianapolis. I was attracted to this work because I have long believed that urban high schools have become places where the majority of students are being underserved. I also know that high schools are the most entrenched of the K–12 cultures and the most resistant to change.

As I think about this latest challenge, I am drawn back to my past experiences, particularly those experiences that were once considered out of the box and cutting edge. I hope I can use my own career experiences in a way that will not only serve the district well, but will strengthen the capacity of the Indianapolis Public Schools to continue the transformation long after the district's current leadership team has moved on.

Clearly (to me, at least), those out-of-the-box experiences that I described above will help to shape my work. But I intend also to search for new out-of-the-box approaches to increase our students' capacity to learn and to improve our faculty's ability to create and facilitate quality knowledge work. I am preparing to launch an extensive quest to enable each teacher, each principal, each small school, each schoolhouse, and the entire district to build the capacity to transform high schools. I will do so armed with the tenets, processes, and experiences learned through IPLA, SIP, SBSD—and other processes that may be as yet unknown to me. The effort and attention to creating capacity is all about creating opportunities for our diverse learners to meet high standards.

Last year, at the National Staff Development Conference, I attended a session led by Al Bertani of Northwestern University. He had served as the director of key reform initiatives in the Chicago Public Schools for several years. I have organized my final comments around a school reform timeline he described in his presentation (see Figure 6.1). Reflecting on his involvement in the transformation of the Chicago Public Schools, he described three waves of school reform he had personally experienced in leading transformational change, beginning in the early 1980s and continuing on into the first part of this century. As I reflected on my own transformation and journey in educational leadership, his time frame struck a chord in me; it mirrored my own experiences.

I agree that a major challenge facing district-level administrators today is building school system capacity that reconciles decentralization and centralization. Key questions we must address include the following:

- How do we reconcile the work of school staff, school councils, the central office, and the board of education so that our work is coherent and connected?
- How do we build professional capacity in our staff?
- How do we reconcile local and central control so that best practice occurs routinely?
- How do we create multiple successful classrooms throughout individual schools and throughout the entire district?

Time Frame	Focus	Driving Force
1983–1998	First wave of reform: **Decentralization** School councils and decentralization of decision making and authority	*A Nation at Risk*
1998–2004	Second wave of reform: **Recentralization** Centralized decision making and central control of NCLB implementation	*NCLB*
2004	Third wave of reform: **Reconciliation** Building capacity for instructional improvement by reconciling decentralization and centralization	*Reality and Best Practice*

Figure 6.1   School Reform Timeline

- How do we create versions of the district's vision in each and every school and classroom?
- How do we create conditions that support the autonomy of building teams to achieve state and local standards?
- How do we create academic rigor without promoting instructional rigor mortis?

I'll need to address these key questions with those I work with, including the superintendent and his key staff, along with community and teacher leaders. The transformation to small high schools has already proven to be problematic in some urban districts. Seattle recently lost its funding from the Gates Foundation when it determined that the Seattle central office and board were not enabling success of small schools, despite the fact that they are community neighbors and that Seattle was one of the first districts awarded Gates money.

The small high school movement in Indianapolis will die on the vine if systematic and simultaneous capacity building is not undertaken soon at both the building and district levels.

The issues faced by Seattle are indicative of the ones we are facing in my new position, as I view the work of a central office that has been carefully designed over many years to perform certain specific functions with efficiency. The small high school movement in Indianapolis will die on the vine if systematic and simultaneous capacity building is not undertaken soon at both the building and district levels.

I have a real sense of urgency as the transformation begins. Will we be able to create the capacity at various levels of the organization to support innovation and improvement? Will we be able to simultaneously build capacity at the individual level, school level, and district level? If so, what structures need to be in place to accomplish this huge task? What values and beliefs must be codified in policy to enable this to occur?

I think our chances will be much better if we adopt proven and tested processes for capacity building that respect and expect out-of-the-box leadership from teachers, principals, district staff, and school board trustees.

NOTES

1.   Indiana Principals Leadership Academy: http://www.doe.state.in.us/ipla/welcome.html

2.   */I/D/E/A/ School Improvement Process.* (1979). Dayton, OH: Author.

3.   /I/D/E/A/ was a nonprofit organization that was organized in the 1970s and disbanded in the early part of this decade.

4.   Schlechty Center for Leadership in School Reform: http://www.schlechtycenter.org/psc/establish.asp

5.   Anderson Community Schools Constitution: http://www.acsc.net/constitution.htm

6.   Schlechty, P. C. (2002). *Working on the work.* San Francisco: Jossey-Bass.

7.   Technoplaza trademark reference: http://www.acsc.net/plaza/home.htm

CHAPTER SEVEN

THROUGH OTHERS' EYES

A Collaborative Model of Leadership

HANK RUBIN

I call them my plate-spinning days.

If you are old enough to remember *The Ed Sullivan Show*, you'll remember the jugglers who balanced spinning plates on the ends of impossibly long wooden poles—sometimes balancing four, five, six, or more plates on poles perched on their noses or chins. That's how I spend my Mondays and Tuesdays.

Mondays I spend in meetings that generally go from 8 AM to 6 PM with my associate dean, department chairs, faculty colleagues on special assignments, internal advisory groups, external advisors, and others with administrative duties in the College of Education and Counseling, plus the vice president and other deans with whom I work at South Dakota State University (SDSU).

Tuesdays I do pretty much the same thing at the University of South Dakota (USD), nearly 110 miles away. I make sure every plate is spinning, in a direction we can agree on, at speeds that make sense and that we can sustain, with the proper people in the proper places with the resources, clarity, and accountability that they and I will need to make sure that all the work of the college will get done—at least for the rest of the week.

As Joint Dean of Education at SDSU and USD (the only joint dean in the nation), I have the responsibilities that every traditional dean has on each campus (including making sure that my units are dependably well managed, excellent in instructional quality, etc.)—and more. I'm charged, too, with building collaborative programs and systems between the two institutions, the expectation of expanding and delivering new programs and services across the state, the obligation of continuously improving the quality of PreK–20 partnerships, and the preparation of teachers, counselors, and administrators in the region.

I was also hired, in part, to be a strong voice for higher education in the region. It's a great job that, in many ways, is not only analogous to that of multisite principals and multidistrict superintendents, but also a somewhat extreme version of the work that *every* educational administrator (from PreK through 20) is expected to perform.

Ours is complicated work that gets done with, through, because of, and sometimes in spite of relationships: relationships with colleagues, with parents, with supervisors, with board members, with businesspeople, with politicians, with agency personnel, with funders, with regulators, with union officials, and with students. I've seen it when I served as associate superintendent for students, families, and communities in the Ohio Department of Education; as a suburban teacher; as an employee of the Chicago Public Schools; as a federal education bureaucrat; and as director of a venerable nonprofit public school watchdog group.

The overarching lesson that I've learned is that it's fundamental to effective leadership to understand that not one of us leads programs, units, school sites, institutions, or district bureaucracies. Each one of us leads *people*—and we lead them in and through relationships.

WHY WE ARE COLLABORATIVE LEADERS

Education's leaders simply don't have an option: We are either *collaborative* leaders or we are not truly effective leaders at all. We do not operate within monolithic closed systems that permit top-down authoritarian control—for any lasting duration, anyway. Nor do we operate within administrative units that control all the forces that directly affect our bottom lines related to student performance and well-being. At best, we influence those who affect our bottom lines. We create opportunities; provide resources; affect cultures; establish and monitor accountability systems; and we influence targets and help align public policies, community resources, and public support that will help us meet the education needs of all our children.

That our work is different from that of our corporate and government counterparts is determined largely by our purpose. Our bottom line is a tapestry of essential and complex public missions— missions that are more diffuse and multifaceted than the bottom lines (such as profit, efficiency, regulatory compliance, etc.) served by most of our corporate and government counterparts. Public education's leaders simply cannot succeed in isolation: we never can be independent operators. We are the advocates, recruiters, and stewards of our public missions. We are successful

Education's leaders simply don't have an option: we are either collaborative leaders or we are not truly effective leaders at all.

to the extent that we build the confidence, vision, and structures needed to support the collaborative relationships that can achieve them.

Let's look at some of the forces that distinguish the work of educational and nonprofit leaders; these forces dictate our use of collaborative—as opposed to authoritarian—practices:

- Our policy boards are richly diverse collections of agendas and people out of which we must build shared visions, goals, and collaborative teams.
- The constituencies we serve are never really homogeneous, even though they may share significant characteristics.
- The culture of education and nonprofits (along with the comparative limitations of our economic resources) puts pressure on our leaders to recruit and engage volunteers for their minds, talents, and access to resources.
- Our reliance on outside funders necessitates strategic alliances that will appeal to the institutional self-interests of diverse agencies and donors.
- Our responsibilities to educate a diverse public and to offer positive direction to elected policymakers necessitate far-reaching, and ever-changing, strategic alliances.

- We are increasingly pushed toward interinstitutional cooperation. Why? Mounting evidence indicates that meeting the
  education, health care, cultural development, and human service needs of children, families, and communities requires a
  comprehensive and integrated approach that can be accomplished only through cooperative relationships with other
  providers.

The challenge we accept as mission-driven leaders of schools
and nonprofits is to become agents of collaboration on behalf of our
missions and to develop the collaborative skills that will enable us
to achieve them. In my 2002 book, *Collaborative Leadership:
Developing Effective Partnerships in Communities and Schools*
(Corwin Press), I laid out the case for principals and superintendents
as collaborative leaders:

> The effective leaders of the 21st century will be *educational
> leaders,* not *school administrators.* They will be community
> leaders operating on behalf of the instructional and learning needs
> of children and their families. They will rally the resources, prick
> the consciences, and focus the energy of individuals and institu-
> tions from every sector of their communities so as to educate their
> children. They will be boundary-spanning advocates and adminis-
> trators for whom "the schools" will be only one locus of their
> work. They will be measured far less by the effectiveness and effi-
> ciency of the administration of their buildings and staffs and far
> more by their ability to rally and sustain the devoted attention and
> resources of their entire community in relationships that meaning-
> fully enhance the educational achievements of their students (per-
> haps reflected, one day, by the things those students accomplish
> long after they have left formal education). . . .
>
> They will be collaborative
> leaders. Follow the workday
> schedule of superintendents and
> principals today, and you will find
> that many already are. (p. 34)

———— ⚜ ————

*The challenge we accept as
mission-driven leaders of schools
and nonprofits is to become agents
of collaboration on behalf of our
missions and to develop the
collaborative skills that will enable
us to achieve them.*

Those of you who are effective
collaborative leaders probably
attribute your success to intuition
or to the influence of one or more

mentors or role models. Unfortunately, few of us can attribute much of our collaborative success to the instructional content of the university programs that prepared us for our positions. That's because so little work has been done to deconstruct and understand what collaborative leadership is all about; to break it into curricular elements—specific skills, knowledge, and dispositions—that can be observed, assessed, and taught. In this chapter, I'll briefly explore a theory of collaborative leadership and apply it to practice in our complex world of educational leadership.

FIRST, DEFINITIONS

Let's begin with a few basic definitions:

- *Collaboration:* A collaboration is a purposeful relationship in which all parties strategically choose to cooperate in order to accomplish a shared outcome. Because of its voluntary nature*, the success of a collaboration depends on a collaborative leader's ability to build and maintain these relationships.
- *Collaborative leader: You* are a collaborative leader once you have accepted responsibility for building—or helping to ensure the success of—a heterogeneous team to accomplish a shared purpose. The *ability to convene and sustain relationships that influence individuals and institutions*—and the ability to find and sustain common self-interests in the diverse missions and goals of independent actors—defines the effective collaborative leader.
- *Relationship management:* Relationship management is what a collaborative leader does. It is the purposeful exercise of behavior, communication, and organizational resources to affect the perspective, beliefs, and behaviors of another person (generally a *collaborative partner*) so as to influence that person's relationship with you and your collaborative enterprise.
- *Collaborative leadership:* Collaborative leadership is the skillful and mission-oriented management of relevant *relationships.*

---

*We can conceive of collaborations that are not voluntary in the strictest sense (an employee may be instructed to lead or contribute to a collaboration that serves the agency's purposes, for example). But they can never be coercive. Coercive collaboration is, at best, subjugation.

A Theory of Collaboration

During the past two-and-a-half decades, with colleagues across the country, I've built, supported, served in, and endured countless collaborative initiatives of almost every imaginable type, size, and quality. In the 1990s—through interviews, reflection, and study—I set out to understand what makes some collaborations successful and others dismal failures; what makes some leaders effective at building and sustaining productive partnerships and others terminally lone wolves.

Today, there are centers, institutes, study groups, and (appropriately) collaboratives that exist to encourage and nurture productive collaborations. What we have long been missing—and what has been the steepest challenge to leadership education—is a unifying theory or model that might guide practice, teaching, and professional development. The theory of collaboration that makes up the rest of this chapter is designed to inform practice, and also to provide useful tools for teachers, administrators, and professors who want to understand, practice, and teach collaborative leadership.

What we have long been missing—and what has been the steepest challenge to leadership education—is a unifying theory or model that might guide practice, teaching, and professional development.

Viewing Collaboration Through Two Lenses

The study and practice of collaboration, like any blend of intellectual pursuit and action, entails both substantive content knowledge and practical application skills. The contribution of a unifying theory should be to help us answer the question, What does a leader need to know and be able to do in order to be a collaborative leader?

On the next few pages, we will look through two lenses:

1. A *systems* lens, through which we will view the larger, or macro, systems in which collaborations occur. In doing so, we'll address the question, What are the forces that shape the environment (and the decisions) of the people with whom

we hope to collaborate? We'll also look at the microsystems that exist within the collaborations in which we participate and provide leadership. In doing so, we'll address this question: What does collaboration look like? Finally, we'll examine the psychological principle that connects—and frequently *dis*connects—individuals and collaborations.

2. A *functional* lens, through which we will view the effective practices of leaders who build and sustain collaborations.

Collaborative leadership happens at the focal point of systems knowledge and effective practice:

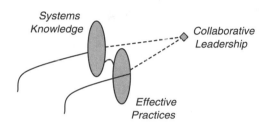

Figure 7.1

SYSTEMS KNOWLEDGE

Collaboration is a relationship, and all relationships are personal. "Interinstitutional collaboration" is a common misnomer: collaboration happens between people. But people are—and carry with them—an enormously complex bundle of systems: gastronomical, neurological, biological, psychological, social, legal, cultural, professional, and more. Understanding systems is essential for understanding why people act as they act and how to influence people's action. *Collaborative leaders are "systems thinkers" who understand that systems are nothing more than mental constructs that improve our effectiveness as relationship managers. Moving systems and moving people are inextricably bound.*

So when collaborative leaders look at collaborative partners, here is a simplified view of what they see:

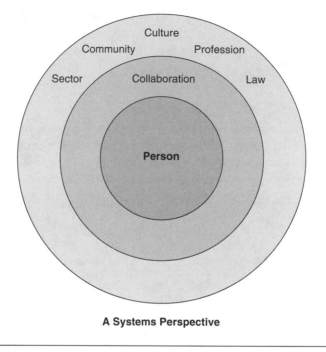

A Systems Perspective

Figure 7.2   A Systems Perspective

Other chapters in this book (and other volumes in this series) address a wide range of leadership issues. Here we will discuss an important and basic psychological principle that either connects or disconnects the person and the collaboration, we will touch on the role of sector knowledge, and then we'll examine a model of collaborative systems.

System: Person

There are three perspectives through which it is possible to observe and understand individuals and the systems in which they function:

- Your perspective as a third-party observer
- The perspective of the prospective partner ("person")
- An objective truth regarding the character of these systems

Arguably, all of these perspectives are valid. For the collaborative leader, however, the most important one is the perspective of the prospective partner. To be effective, collaborative leaders work to see the world—surrounding systems, the issue that gives rise to the collaboration, and even the collaborative leader him- or herself—through the eyes of their collaborative partners.

The key principle here is reminiscent of Gandhi's style of leadership: "There go my people; I must follow them because I am their leader." As a general rule, people don't willingly follow leaders in order to serve the leaders' interests; they freely follow when their own interests are being served. And, because people define their interests (and their identities) through their own understanding of their relationships with the systems that surround them, leaders who can see the world through others' eyes are best able to (1) articulate the collaborative issue in a fashion that connects it to the self-interests of prospective partners and (2) build collaborative relationships with these partners that are effective because they respect, support, and align with the systems in which these partners already see themselves operating.

As a general rule, people don't willingly follow leaders in order to serve the leaders' interests; they freely follow when their own interests are being served.

System: Sectors

More often than not, the partners with whom we work in collaborations are representing more than their own self-interests. Whether they are teachers, counselors, administrators, parents, businesspeople, funders, or state department regulators, many are in the collaboration as the delegate or representative of a group—or they see themselves as having some kind of representational responsibility. These partners see the collaboration as a vehicle for accomplishing something for their groups, and we need to know what that something is.

Moreover, such representative partners carry into the collaboration not only specific goals from their home groups; they also come with policies, politics, reporting relationships, time frames for getting things done, and other external influences that shape what they expect from the collaboration, how they view it, and how they operate within it.

Consider this example, which principals and superintendents who work with business groups will recognize. When working with entrepreneurial for-profit businesspeople who are used to decisions being made quickly on the basis of clear-cut bottom-line criteria, the most comfortable and productive collaborative environment is apt to be one that is fast-paced, formal, quantitative, and on time, perhaps

starting at 6 AM before the workday begins. On the other hand, partnerships involving teachers, counselors, and nonprofit people are
more apt to be effective if they are participatory, mission-driven,
open to expression of opinions and needs, and begin before dinner,
shortly after the school day ends. And collaborations involving
parents and working volunteers—with day jobs and families—are
probably best scheduled at around 7:30 PM, after dinner and homework and slightly before exhaustion sets in.

No administrator working in the principalship or superintendency works only with people employed inside the school or just
with district staff. Today's educational leaders routinely cross
boundaries to collaborate with private, for-profit, governmental,
nonprofit, philanthropic, regulatory, and volunteer colleagues. This
makes the respect that is born of knowledge about others and their
contexts all the more important.

We respect people who respect us. And no right-minded person
would willingly volunteer to partner with a collaborative leader
whose behavior or lack of knowledge suggests disrespect. But, in the
stereotypic shorthand to which we all fall victim, educators and nonprofit people have little respect for the self-serving ruthlessness of
businesspeople, businesspeople have little respect for the mushy
soft-headedness of soft-hearted educators and nonprofit people, and
no one respects the heartlessness and blundering inefficiency of government bureaucrats. As someone who has served in all three roles,
I promise any doubters that these stereotypes are no more true of the
other sectors than they are of yours.

To be effective collaborative leaders, we don't need to be expert
in the legal, social, historical, and cultural elements of the professions, organizations, and sectors from which our collaborative
colleagues come. But we do need working insights so as to be
knowledgeable of the institutional contexts that shape our partners'
interests and perspectives as they work with us in the collaboration.
Effective collaborative leaders not only reach beyond the limits of
their own organizations, they also reach across professions and
across the boundaries that define the education/nonprofit, government, and for-profit sectors. Most of us need to expand our limited
knowledge of others' professions and sectors in order to find our

---— ⚘ ——---

*Effective collaborative leaders not
only reach beyond the limits of
their own organizations, they also
reach across professions and
across boundaries.*

mutual self-interests, to build effective relationships, and to understand the conditions that affect the decisions and needs of our collaborative partners.

System: Collaboration

Collaboration is a dynamic and evolving system of relationships. While most collaborations are purposeful (with definitive beginnings and endings), some seem to simply emerge and recede, functioning when needed and lying dormant otherwise. By developing a theoretical model of *collaboration's life cycle,* we can examine its organic nature, explore the phases through which any collaboration is prone to grow, and develop tools for assessing and projecting its progress over time. Here is a model to explore briefly from your perspective as a collaborative leader.

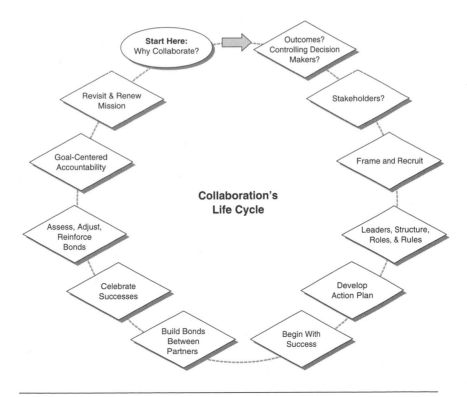

Figure 7.3   Collaboration's Life Cycle

The life cycle begins with a basic question:

- *Why Collaborate?* Often, collaboration is more difficult and time-consuming than its alternative. The very first phase entails fundamental questions: What do you really want to achieve? Is the goal best achieved through collaboration? Have you carefully considered the questions of how and why a collaborative approach improves the likelihood of accomplishing your goals?
- *Outcomes? Decision Makers?* What are the targeted outcomes? Who are the essential decision makers? Did you take the time to refine your thinking about your general goal(s) so that the outcomes you hope to target are clear enough to make it possible for you to identify *by name* the decision makers who control or influence your ability to succeed? When decision makers *who were not likely to participate* were selected, did you identify alternatives—for example, individuals who (1) directly influence the other decision makers, (2) are themselves desirable members of the coalition, and (3) are likely to respond favorably to recruitment?
- *Stakeholders?* Who are the stakeholders who need to be involved? Did you identify *by name* the full range of essential stakeholders, individuals, and organizations with knowledge, history, celebrity, credibility, influence, or resources, or who otherwise have a stake in the outcome(s) you are targeting?
- *Frame and Recruit.* Did you develop a unique, tailored strategy to recruit each prospective partner? Did your preplanning include consideration of who—from the perspective of each prospective partner—should make the overture and what— again, from the perspective of each prospective partner—will satisfy the prospect's self-interests and make him or her enthusiastic about participating in your collaboration? Has attention been paid to engage each partner in (1) discussing and reaching at least some general agreement on the mission and goals of the collaboration, and (2) solidifying the connection of each partner's self-interests with the emerging mission and operation of the collaboration?
- *Leaders, Structure, Roles, and Rules.* Has there been reflection on the question of whether formalization of leadership, structure, functional roles, and operating rules would help or hurt the collaborative process? Has the collaboration

strategically moved toward formality, with an effort to ensure that all partners are comfortable with and invested in the leadership, structure, roles, and rules? Or did the collaboration move too abruptly or prematurely, scaring away some partners who might have contributed but who may not have felt adequately connected to the collaboration or supported by their organizations to formally commit to the work? Were routine meeting dates established for the collaboration? Have routine communications been developed and deployed to keep all essential players informed of the coalition's work?

- *Develop an Action Plan.* Did the collaboration develop strategic plans with benchmarks so that all its members know where the collaboration is going and can measure how far it's come? Have partners been encouraged to discuss the collaboration's action plan in terms of how specific portions connect to the institutional missions and self-interests that they represent?
- *Begin With Successes.* Did the collaboration begin with short-term plans that targeted successes around either its most urgent or least controversial goal(s)? Has the collaboration's action plan been built on such early successes?
- *Build Bonds Between Partners.* How has the collaboration paid attention to building the essential bonds between collaborative partners? Has an internal environment of trust, loyalty, and high professionalism been created early on so that, later, partners are willing to make the compromises that will certainly be demanded in the context of collaborative decision making?
- *Celebrate Successes.* What has been done to make sure that collaborative partners feel good about their continued participation in the collaboration? Has the collaboration celebrated its successes with internal recognitions to strengthen these bonds? Has external publicity been used as a tool to build momentum, support, and pride among partners and key external constituencies?

> *What has been done to make sure that collaborative partners feel good about their continued participation in the collaboration? Has the collaboration celebrated its successes?*

- *Assess, Adjust, and Reinforce Bonds.* Do leaders really know if individual partners feel connected to and supportive of the collaboration? How does this collaboration routinely measure, adjust, and reinforce the bonds between collaborative partners?
- *Goal-Centered Accountability.* How does the collaboration measure its progress toward goals? Does it have clear indicators of success? Are these indicators known to all members of the collaboration? Are they reviewed and updated routinely? How does what is measured relate to what is done?
- *Revisit and Renew Mission.* Are the collaboration's partners aware of and routinely reminded of the mission and goals of the collaboration? Does the collaboration stop to revisit its mission, especially at significant benchmarks? Is the collaboration flexible enough to explore the pros and cons of all possible options, including (1) modifying the mission or operating ground rules, (2) retaining them intact, (3) expanding or redirecting the mission, (4) taking a vacation, or (5) disbanding?

EFFECTIVE PRACTICE

This is the lens through which we observe and measure the characteristics represented in the work and among the leaders of successful collaborations.

Twenty-four dimensions have emerged. While it's not likely that all the skills, knowledge, and dispositions described in these dimensions (outlined below) will reside in any one leader, they become our targets for professional development and the characteristics to be sought in the partners we recruit. They are starting points for self- (and group) assessment, targets for self- (and group) improvement, and an outline of the competencies around which we may begin to build curricula for teaching the skills of collaborative leadership.

- **Systems Thinking:** Collaborative leaders view their world as the complex interaction of systems: people within organizations within coalitions within communities, and so forth. In general, collaborative leadership exists in the process of aligning these systems toward shared outcomes.

- **Strategic Thinking:** The effective collaborative leader is a strategic, logical, and systemic thinker who understands the steps that must be taken to make things happen and who can engage collaborative partners in a productive, efficient planning process.

- **Asset-Based Perspective:** Collaborative leaders see assets to be aligned where others see disjointed resources and players. They help others see and share a vision of what can be accomplished together where others see a problem to be overcome. They see assets as the foundation upon which sustained collaborations are built. An asset-based perspective shapes both the dialogue between partners and the targets that they set.

- **Professional Credibility:** Collaborative leaders must have professional credibility; otherwise, few professional colleagues will join with them. Before most professionals will agree to join a portion of their visions and reputations in partnership with a collaborative leader, they will judge their confidence in that leader. Credibility/confidence is earned by having (1) substantive mastery, (2) peer status, and (3) professional integrity.

- **Timing the Launch:** Whether a collaboration is launched in response to a crisis or in order to plan and carry out a long-standing vision, the timing of its launch will influence who comes on board and how best to organize the initiative. The very fact that the dynamic interplay of systems can make this dimension unpredictable (who, for instance, could have predicted the social effects of Hurricane Katrina in the city of New Orleans?) highlights the need for both strategic and flexible leadership at every stage of the collaboration.

- **Recruiting the Right Mix:** Nothing shapes the culture, process, and outcomes of a collaborative initiative as much as decisions related to who is asked to join it. This is an intensely strategic dimension, which must address considerations that include stakeholders, decision makers, and the distribution of these 24 dimensions within the profiles of a collaboration's recruits.

- **Interpersonal Communication Skills:** Communication sits at the center of all human relationships. Collaboration, as relationship management, demands the skillful use of interpersonal communication. *Successful* collaborations maintain a climate in which honest and productive communication is nurtured among partners.

- **Consensus Building:** Consensus building connects the individual and institutional self-interests of partners to the goals and activities of the collaboration. Some collaborations work well on a consensus model; some succeed with a majoritarian model. Within either model, it is *always* beneficial in public-sector collaborations for leaders to have the skills to build the largest possible consensus around action before it is taken.

- **Diplomacy:** It is safe to say that few people will sacrifice the good of their home organizations for the benefit of an external collaboration. The diplomatic function of a collaborative leader is to strike an ongoing balance between the competing and evolving interests of individual members (and the interests of their groups or organizations as they see them) with the interests of the collaboration as a whole.

- **Understanding the Rudiments of Each Sector:** As noted earlier, virtually no educational leader works exclusively with colleagues and constituents who come only from education. Most of us need to expand our limited knowledge of others' professions and sectors so as to help us find mutual self-interests, build effective relationships, and understand the conditions that affect the decisions and needs of our collaborative partners.

- **Data-Driven Leadership:** In the twenty-first century, data rule. Technology, standards, and mandated accountability are unrelenting taskmasters that drive leaders and educators to numbers, research, and best practices.

- **Psychosocial: Understanding People:** The most elemental skill required of collaborative leaders is the interpersonal skill and empathy needed to make and sustain strong linkages between people. The tools begin with a built-in radar that detects the personal self-interests people bring into a relationship, that deduces each person's level of commitment to the relationship, and that observes and interprets the relevant psychosocial rhythms and styles of each individual. This leadership challenge is more

---

The most elemental skill required of collaborative leaders is the interpersonal skill and empathy needed to make and sustain strong linkages between people.

complicated for collaborative leaders, who are not only dealing with individuals as complex psychosocial organisms, but also as social beings who often are representatives of complex groups with highly individualized structures, needs, histories, and *institutional* self-interests.

- **Institutionalizing the Worry:** This is, perhaps, the most undervalued, often ignored, and important dimension of collaborative leadership. It is the dimension that guarantees that somebody is worried about the success of the collaboration, so that the collaboration will not disintegrate for lack of attention. It is a self-possessed tenacity on the part of the collaborative leader, making sure that the collaborative venture is fed, nourished, and attended to during each phase of its development. It is figuratively—if not formally—written into the job description of the collaborative leader or some delegated agent. It is the practical response to the acknowledged truth that if no one person accepts responsibility for the success of any process, cause, project, or collaborative initiative, then surely it will be displaced to lower and lower levels on everyone's list of priorities until, at last, it disappears altogether.

- **Group Process:** The effective collaborative leader is (1) an environmental engineer; (2) a group facilitator; and, all too often, (3) a grunt worker. Each of these functions is essential for an atmosphere that encourages cohesion, efficiency, and productivity.

- **Resource Development:** This is a straightforward dimension of any contemporary leadership post, but it is more complicated when applied to collaborations because of our responsibility to enhance the capacity of our collaborative partners and to never hurt or impede their ability to raise the resources they need for their home institutions. (In other words, raising funds for a collaborative initiative should never compete with—and should often contribute to—the resource development goals of the collaboration's partners.)

- **Marketing/Communications:** Marketing is the planned and managed dialogue among a corporate entity's internal and external decision makers, stakeholders, and customers. "Communications" is the name we give to the same function in the public sector. Our job as collaborative leaders is to make sure that this dialogue is productive, timely, and inclusive.

- **Technological Savvy:** Desktop and Internet technology make communication spontaneous, easy, accessible, and cheap. Technology makes collaboration possible at tremendous speed, efficiency, and breadth.
- **Managerial Skill:** Collaborative leaders are called upon to be effective and efficient managers of their organizations as well as of their collaborations. This is very simple; educational leaders whose schools or districts are poorly managed probably won't be around long enough to see the fruits of their collaborative leadership.
- **Entrepreneurism:** Collaborative leaders are always creating, adapting, and innovating in order to establish and maintain their relationships with the individuals and institutions associated with their collaborations. The notion of entrepreneurism—as a persistently innovative, evolving strategy—is a key element of relationship management.
- **Vision-Centered Leadership:** At every decision-making juncture, the question on the mind of collaborative leaders is, "Does this help us achieve our goal(s)?" As their collaborations' institutional worriers and strategic thinkers, the job of collaborative leaders is to ensure that each step their group takes advances it toward shared goal(s). When partners wander, get distracted, or slow down, it's up to collaborative leaders to raise the rallying vision like a flag to sustain the focus and momentum of the collaboration.
- **Integrity:** Collaboration is like marriage, with a courtship during which the intentions and integrity of both parties are tested until each is satisfied that a commitment is safe and warranted. Mutual confidence in the integrity of the partnership and of each partner is a prerequisite for any long-term commitment.

> *Collaboration is like marriage, with a courtship during which the intentions and integrity of both parties are tested until each is satisfied that a commitment is safe and warranted.*

- **Spirituality:** Collaborative leaders interact with and influence the spirit and world view of those who join the collaboration. On the surface, such leaders are expected to radiate an energy of achievability—a "can-do" attitude—that generates a confidence among partners that the time they are investing will yield results. At a deeper level, within the context of the collaboration, collaborative leaders nurture a culture of coherent values, commitment to egalitarian principles, and belief in the Tocquevillian observation that we accomplish more good together than we ever could alone.

- **Commitment to Diversity:** Collaborative leaders are aware of both the political and functional imperatives of diversity: Diversity makes collaborations more legitimate and intelligent. On the one hand, collaborations whose members don't reflect the cultural, religious, and racial diversity that comprise the systems and constituencies in which they operate run the immediate (and fatal) risk of being dysfunctionally isolated, illegitimate, unresponsive, or worse. At the same time, collaborations that don't represent a diversity of opinions, perspectives, and resources are fatally narrow, monolithic, and limited in capacity. Like a chorus that doesn't harmonize the different ranges, timbres, and tones of its voices, such a group is little more than a somewhat louder version of a single voice singing.

- **Charisma:** Effective collaborative leaders exude a special type of charisma that attracts and sustains the emotional desire of others to work with them. But never confuse charisma with dynamism. Charismatic leaders are not necessarily dynamic, although they might be. What makes effective collaborative leaders charismatic is the ability to attract and sustain the emotional desire of other people to *want* to work with them—to like working with them. It is connected to integrity, dependability, and a general can-do optimism but is really an affective quality that is hard to define and can only be observed—and, therefore, taught—through the eyes of other people.

THE CONCEPTUAL FRAMEWORK

If collaborative leadership happens at the focal point of systems knowledge and effective practice, then the most instructive contribution of this theory will be its ability to predict and provide guidance on the correlation and contribution of each of these dimensions to the success of a collaboration at each phase of its life cycle. This next explorational step can be described as *a conceptual framework for collaborative leadership;* it is portrayed by the following table:

Table 7.1

A Conceptual Framework for Collaborative Leadership

Dimensions of Collaborative Leadership	Why Collaborate?	Outcomes? Decision Makers?	Stakeholders?	Frame and Recruit	Leaders, Structure, Roles, & Rules	Develop Action Plan	Begin With Success	Build Bonds Between Partners	Celebrate Successes	Assess, Adjust, Reinforce Bonds	Goal-Centered Accountability	Revisit & Renew Mission
Systems Thinking												
Strategic Thinking												
Asset-Based Perspective												
Professional Credibility												
Timing the Launch												
Recruiting the Right Mix												
Interpersonal Communication Skills												
Consensus Building												
Diplomacy												
Understanding the Rudiments of Each Sector												
Data-Driven Leadership												
Psychosocial: Understanding People												
Institutionalizing the Worry												
Group Process												
Resource Development												
Marketing/Communications												
Technological Savvy												
Managerial Skill												
Entrepreneurism												
Vision-Centered Leadership												
Integrity												
Spirituality												
Commitment to Diversity												
Charisma												

COLLABORATIVE LESSONS

Until theory is tested and proven, there is much we can learn—and that we *have* learned—from reflection and experience. Over the years, the successes and failures of collaborative leaders have yielded some consistent predictors of success and insights to effective collaborative practice. Here are seven principles that have been found time after time in collaborations that work. I hope you won't view these principles as a summary, or even a comprehensive overview, of this chapter . . . but they are important.

Cultivate a shared vision right from the start, even if it's vague.

Take care to *recruit the right mix* to reach your stakeholders and decision makers.

Become—or ensure that you have identified—the *institutional worrier.* This is the person who will pay unwavering attention to sustaining the momentum and attending to the management details of the collaboration, along with engaging the perspectives and addressing the process needs of each individual partner in the work of the collaboration.

Work to *see the world through the eyes of those you would lead.* This will help you see how to ensure that each partner's *individual and institutional self-interests are served* by both the process and products of the collaboration.

Don't waste time. Meetings must be efficient and productive; management must be lean and driven. Remember that for everyone else this is no more than a second priority.

Routinize the structure and the roster of participants. Make the collaboration a regular item on participants' schedules. Recognize that it is easier and more popular to cancel a meeting or to remove a responsibility than it is to add a meeting or responsibility to participants' lives. Secure commitments from all participants that every possible effort will be made to ensure that the same people come to the table each time

> *"Interinstitutional collaboration" is a misnomer. Effective collaboration happens between people—one person at a time.*

the collaboration meets. Scarcely anything stifles creativity, productivity, and commitment more than wasting time each meeting bringing a new delegate "up to speed."

All collaboration is personal. Cultivating partners shouldn't end
once they commit to the partnership. Cultivation of partners'
attachment to the collaboration requires ongoing attention.
"Interinstitutional collaboration" is a misnomer. Effective collaboration happens *between people—one person at a time.*

Every day, every adult will decide dozens of times whether to enthu-
siastically follow, passively comply with, tacitly resist, or actively
reject the panoply of leaders—from our nation's president to our
local principal—who try to influence each of our lives. We make
these decisions on the basis of either compulsion (i.e., we just don't
have any choice), faith in the leader (i.e., we believe in the leader's
integrity and competence, even if we don't agree with his or her
direction), or self-interest (i.e., by following this leader we will get
something we value that we would not get otherwise).

All of us in education know that the only thing we can *compel* is
students' attendance up to a certain age, and even that doesn't work
very well when the students' interests aren't being served. So our
effectiveness as education's leaders is predicated on our *integrity, competence,* and *ability to connect to our various partners' self-interests.*
And none of these characteristics can be faked. These are the characteristics that spell the success or failure of every public leader. Every
plate we spin—and every partnership we build—in our schools,
universities, communities, and country challenges us to be collaborative leaders with integrity, competence, empathy, authenticity, and
persistence.

CHAPTER EIGHT

EMBRACING THE ENEMY

Moving Beyond the Pain of Leadership

JEROME T. MURPHY

Near the end of a wrenching discussion about sleepless nights, all eyes turned to an esteemed superintendent who had remained quiet during this monthly meeting of peers. Responding to his fellow superintendents, he declared with seeming bravado, "Hey, I sleep like a baby." Then, hesitantly, he dropped his mask of control and continued with a hitch in his voice, "I sometimes sleep for a few hours, and then I wake up crying. Just like the old joke says."[1]

Not every leader sheds tears over the pressures and demands of leadership, but I've come to believe that it is common for even the most competent and well-adjusted managers to experience real psychological pain—even suffering—on the job. Certainly, more than

Author's Note: I'd like to thank Tom Champion, Barry Jentz, Jean Murphy, Nancy Murphy, Samantha Tan and especially Ari Betof for their very helpful comments on this chapter. I'd also like to acknowledge that this work would have been impossible without the benefit of ongoing conversations with Ronald Heifetz and Barry Jentz.

once during my 17 years as associate dean and then dean of the Harvard Graduate School of Education, I was overwhelmed by the struggles of leading. The work of leadership can be wonderfully rewarding—indeed, it has been the most invigorating part of my career—but pain is part of the deal. Unfortunately, many of us just don't know how to handle it.

In this chapter, I intend to speculate about the psychological pain of leadership. By pain, I have in mind the *Free Dictionary*'s definition: "emotional distress—a fundamental feeling that people try to avoid." I'll examine some of the major sources of leadership pain, hypothesize about common dysfunctional responses, and look at productive ways for managers to move beyond the pain of leadership. Unlike the other authors in this volume, my goal is not to think "outside the box" of leadership, but rather to shine a light *inside* the box—in this case, the Pandora's box that holds the inner struggles and personal demons of senior managers.

My goal is not to think "outside the box" of leadership, but rather to shine a light inside *the box—in this case, the Pandora's box that holds the inner struggles and personal demons of senior managers.*

Instead of controlling pain, I propose that we embrace what we have, since childhood, thought of as the enemy. I propose that we accept our internal pain and selectively reveal our emotions, and also that we divert our energy and attention to changing what we can in the external world. Through acceptance, we can play the cards that life has dealt us; in the process, pain may morph into just another card in our hand. Through the selective revealing of our emotions, we can build trust and credibility as well as show our humanity—implicitly giving others permission to do the same. Through changing our behavior, we can help achieve our goals and live our values.

I suggest that pain is widespread not only because managers are human, but also because of the unique nature and demands of managerial work, coupled with our culture's larger-than-life conceptions of leadership. Pain is important, too, because so many managers try to control it (privately as well as publicly)—and in the process turn pain into an enemy to fight, flee, or avoid. My hypothesis is that this focus on pain as the enemy is counterproductive—that it engenders even more pain and suffering, and can cause us to fall short as leaders. I further suggest that this topic has been a neglected subject of inquiry and discussion precisely because pain itself is a taboo topic. Leaders are supposed to be strong. We are conditioned to believe that acknowledging pain, even to ourselves, is a sign of weakness.

The ideas that form the heart of this chapter have deep roots in many source materials—from the ancient wisdom of Buddhism to modern thinking about psychotherapy, from old scholarship about military strategy to new musings about leadership.[2] I also draw heavily from conversations with valued colleagues, and from my personal observations and experience. Indeed, inspired by the superintendent in the opening vignette, I too will drop my mask, at least a little, and use examples from my decanal past to illustrate managerial fear and anxiety. (To make this unmasking a little easier for myself, I have fastened a note to the top right corner of my computer monitor, on which I've written "courage.")

In part, I hope to stimulate research that will test my speculations. My guess is that coping with pain is a significant problem for many managers, but not for all. (In my case, I loved being a dean *and* also needed help from a leadership consultant to address the emotional toll exacted by the work.[3]) It seems to me that knowing how the numbers break down and understanding the contours of the problem are worthy topics for deeper investigation. In the meantime, I hope this chapter will help managers notice and acknowledge their pain, recognize that it's perfectly normal to have pain, and learn some new ways to address it. And I hope to help provoke legitimate practitioner-talk about how to manage the emotional distress of being an educational leader today. The opening story hints at the intensity of the problem and the personal costs of covering up the struggle.

LEADING IS PAINFUL

Ordinary life can be filled with excitement and joy—and it can also be filled, as we all know, with pain and suffering: the loss of a parent; disturbing memories about growing up; your child's shame at failing at sports; the sudden sickness of your beloved sister; a bitter fight within your family; worries about paying college bills; a sense of helplessness in controlling your destiny. Each of us has a different list, and our lists go on and on. Experiencing emotional distress—and finding the means to handle it—is a fundamental part of being human.

I believe that these too-familiar pains of ordinary life are ampli-fied in high-stakes leadership positions. For one thing, ordinary mortals don't check their humanity at the office door. Indeed, for many managers, their office is their second home, and their work-mates are their second families. For another, the responsibilities of leadership present significant new sources of distress, which are exacerbated because these moments of trial and tribulation are often put on public display.

Linda Hill has studied the life of first-time managers, who describe their initial year in their new job as a period of surprising emotional upheaval—more debilitating and overwhelming than they had ever imagined. Some "spoke of insomnia, low-grade headaches, back pain, and increased arguments." One confided, "I never knew a promotion could be so painful."[4]

While a new management job can be particularly stressful, Hill contends that the roots of leadership pain grow out of four enduring features of managerial work:

- The "role strain" caused by the overload, uncertainty, and conflict
- The drumbeat of negativity resulting from problems con-stantly dumped on the manager's desk
- The isolation—and loneliness—of authority ("I'm no longer one of the boys," said one manager. "No one asks me out for lunch. No one gossips with me. I'm alone.")
- The "burdens of leadership"—making thorny trade-offs, the weight of being a role model, and wielding power over people's lives[5]

Edgar Schein adds to Hill's list by pointing to the pivotal role played by "learning anxiety" in organizational change:

Learning anxiety comes from being afraid to try something new for fear that it will be too difficult, that we will look stupid in the attempt, or that we will have to part from old habits that have worked for us in the past. Learning something new can cast us as the deviant in the groups we belong to. It can threaten our self-esteem and, in extreme cases, even our identity.[6]

Learning lies at the heart of leading. Thus, to be a leader means that we must manage our own anxiety, as well as the anxiety of others.

These painful aspects of leadership are significantly increased when a leader promotes transformative change, as Ronald Heifetz and Marty Linsky argue:

Let's face it, to lead is to live dangerously. While leadership is often depicted as an exciting and glamorous endeavor, one in which you inspire others to follow you through good times and bad, such a portrayal ignores leadership's dark side: the inevitable attempts to take you out of the game.[7]

As leaders, we will be undercut, they argue, because people "want to be comfortable again, and you're in the way." We can expect personal attacks, marginalization, and efforts to divert us from our goals. We can also expect to experience our own fear of losing our supporters' approval and affection.[8]

Even if we're not knocked out of the game, as educational leaders we are working at the frontier of social change, where it is easy to make mistakes and where our every move and utterance is scrutinized closely. Expectations are high; the margin for error becomes slimmer every day. Inevitably, we will

As educational leaders we are working at the frontier of social change, where it is easy to make mistakes and where our every move and utterance is scrutinized closely.

- fail in finding the right strategies to meet the high expectations of a key constituency group;
- make an occasional public gaffe—a flippant remark, a stupid organizational mistake;
- renege on commitments in the face of competing demands;
- be caught off guard and flummoxed as we struggle with a turbulent world;
- be misunderstood—and unable to respond because of confidential information;
- be rejected in our efforts to promote change or adopt new approaches.

In the wake of these realities, it is easy for many managers to feel overwhelmed, fearful, disappointed, helpless, angry—and just plain awful. It is easy to feel unappreciated for our valiant efforts in defying the odds. In an environment where perfect pitch is expected and false notes amplified, the threat of feeling (and looking) like a fool—embarrassed and humiliated—is always lurking.

As if these sources of pain were not enough, the responsibility of educational leadership can also create anguish because of the gap between our dreams for children and how children are too often treated by society. It is certainly easy for me to become outraged, frustrated, indignant, and overwrought. Over many years, I have found that I need help to know how to deal with these feelings—and so, I suspect, do many other leaders.

Finally, to top it all off, many managers compound their pain—I know I did—by a never-ending internal dialogue in which we beat ourselves up with "should have, could have" evaluations of our agonizing predicament.

Of course, I'd be the first to acknowledge that this somber look at leadership is one-sided. Leading can be an exhilarating experience and a lot of fun—and, in my experience, well worth the effort. But as Heifetz and Linsky remind us, "The harsh truth is that it is not possible to know the rewards and joys of leading without experiencing the pain as well."[9]

COPING BY CONTROLLING

While it's apparent that leadership can be painful, it's a lot less obvious how managers typically cope with it. Here I examine two dimensions of coping: how managers *experience* pain and how they *express* it. I speculate that many managers muddle through by trying to control their pain privately and hide it publicly.

Control behavior takes several overlapping forms. Perhaps the most recognizable is suppression. Painful feelings are simply kept in check. We won't allow ourselves to feel sad after firing a friend, feel distraught after botching a decision, or feel unappreciated after being taken for granted. We control our pain, so the clichés go, by sweeping our negative feelings under the rug, putting a lid on them, or bottling them up. These clichés capture a lot more truth than is usually acknowledged.

A related way to control pain is to escape the problem causing it—after all, eliminating trouble (a.k.a. problem solving) is a central activity of management, and most people are promoted to management positions because they are first-class problem solvers.[10]

So, when it comes to internal troubles, managers routinely apply the same techniques. We break loose of our confusion by quickly fixing the situation causing it. We free ourselves of our anxiety by making a snap decision rather than enduring a painful meeting. We get rid of our anger by withdrawing from the conflict situation.

A first cousin of escape is avoidance, and leaders learn a variety of methods to stay out of harm's way. We steer clear of the anxiety of learning by becoming risk-averse. We distance ourselves from the pain of interpersonal conflict by remaining aloof. We protect ourselves from the agony of possible failure by holding back from making a commitment. We fend off feeling helpless in meeting high expectations by becoming distracted by our lowly status as educators. We avoid the pain of leadership—and make ourselves feel important—by focusing our energies on exploiting the trappings of leadership: a big office, time for travel, an expense account, a designated parking space.

Over time, our control mechanisms can morph into learned numbness. We develop a thick skin to deaden biting criticism. We turn to dark humor and sarcasm to deflect the slings and arrows of leadership. We replace optimism with cynicism.

Over time, these control mechanisms can morph into learned numbness. We develop a thick skin to deaden biting criticism. We turn to dark humor and sarcasm to deflect the slings and arrows of leadership. We replace optimism with cynicism. Worn down, we learn to cope with the relentless pain of work by becoming callous and emotionally comatose.[11]

In addition to taking private steps to control pain, managers find ways to hide their pain while at the office and in other public venues. One of the most common ways of hiding pain is to use the mask of calm and confidence—and cheerfulness. We may be rattled by a sudden crisis, but if asked we would definitely deny it. We may be drowning under the pressure of high expectations, but we certainly are not going to show it. We may be feeling like a complete failure, but we are not going to discuss it. Of the new managers Hill interviewed, many were "reluctant to mention the extent of their upset, even to their spouses" (see endnote 4).

As dean, I remember chairing a spring faculty meeting, which couldn't be postponed, while outside a group of angry students were demonstrating against school policies. The students were chanting, playing drums, and blocking the street—all in an effort to be heard. Not knowing what to do, and churning inside, I chaired the meeting with a strained smile and tried to act as if I were in control! A former principal calls this pattern "the art of the bluff." Looking back, I call it a missed opportunity.

There are, without doubt, many managers out there who don't engage in these coping strategies of suppression, escape, avoidance, learned numbness, and denial. Yet I know that I did as dean—and my guess is that this control behavior is a lot more prevalent than we would like to admit. Certainly, the pattern of managers hiding their feelings at the office, in the name of professionalism, is widespread.

PAIN AS THE ENEMY

Consider this puzzle: Why will some of us do nearly anything to control the feelings and thoughts that cause us pain? To be sure, pain is a bummer for anyone but blissful masochists. Yet the reason goes deeper than simply that pain is a pain. I propose that many managers persist in seeing pain as an absolute enemy because they believe that feeling pain is a sign that they are doing something wrong. Athletes may distinguish between the inevitable pain of exertion that builds new muscle and the warning pain of injury, but pain is all the same to many managers—and it's all bad. "The meaning of pain," says Barry Jentz, "is failure to most of us."[12]

Many of us have grown up learning that distressing feelings and thoughts are bad things to be escaped and avoided. We have been taught to feel good, be happy and nice, and think positively about others and ourselves. Particularly in Westernized societies, we have been carefully educated to control our emotions.

> *I propose that many managers persist in seeing pain as an absolute enemy because they believe that feeling pain is a sign that they are doing something wrong.*

As an example, remember that "the little boy who cries on the playground is told, 'Pull yourself together; don't be a baby'," according to Georg Eifert and Steven Forsyth. "Through these and other experiences, children and adults learn to regulate their experiences and expression of their emotions." They continue, "Emotional regulation is used as evidence of maturity, health and wellness, success, fulfillment, and happiness."[13] If we don't control our emotions, in short, we will fail to measure up to societal expectations.

I contend that this learned propensity to control our emotions is amplified for managers because of widely accepted expectations for leadership. Leaders are supposed to be strong, tough, and decisive—to have all the answers. Leaders are supposed to be in control. (The headline for the lead story on the front page of this morning's *New York Times* declares, "Roberts Is at Court's Helm, But He Isn't Yet in Control."[14] The new chief justice of the Supreme Court, in other words, has yet to meet expectations.) As leaders, we are supposed to control our work and also control our emotions. We are expected to be winners, not whiners.

It is quite remarkable that, despite all that has been written debunking the superhuman qualities of leadership, the myth of the solitary, heroic leader at the top endures. This image still holds astonishing sway in the minds of both the public and many managers. Given these superhuman expectations, it is not surprising that we lapse into negative self-evaluations and conclude that we don't measure up as a leader. In our hyperactive minds, some of us even create what I call the Measure Up Monster[15]—MUM for short—that emerges from its cave waggling a censorious claw in our faces as we struggle to do a good job. In our darkest moments, MUM is always there voicing criticism and abuse:

- "You let that silly remark get to you? What a weakling!"
- "Leaders don't get lost—you're an impostor!"
- "What a wimp! Can't make up your own mind."

At the office, MUM has a ready response to every problem, telling us we have no business feeling pain, and thereby making the pain even worse:

- When an unexpected event baffles you, MUM says, "Bluff, or you'll look stupid!"
- When a defeat leaves you feeling crushed, MUM has little sympathy: "Buck up. You'll lose face."
- When your staff's behavior infuriates you, MUM tells you to keep it to yourself: "Careful. Don't make a bad situation worse!"

So we allow MUM to dictate our actions, and we remain mum at the office. MUM doesn't make us feel better; we feel helpless in its clutches.

The might of MUM no doubt differs among managers. But given the superhuman expectations for leadership and the ease with which we can fall short, it is hardly surprising that some of us see our pain as the enemy. After all, pain is not just a plain vanilla annoyance, but rather a harsh signal—and a reminder—that we are a flop as a leader. Added to our pain, then, is our dread of MUM leaving its cave and waving its poisonous talons. So we keep our MUM cornered in its cave by controlling our enemy—and burying our pain at the office.

Or so my speculation goes—not to mention my professional experience.

THE SOLUTION BECOMES THE PROBLEM

For those of us who struggle with pain and the meanings we attach to it, it seems only natural to try to control it. After all, control works in solving problems in the physical world: If you are about to be run over by a bus, you skedaddle out of the way. The problem is that control doesn't work in the psychological arena, at least in the long run. Paradoxically, the more we attempt to control our pain, the more we twist ourselves into knots and undermine our effectiveness.

The problem with the control strategy is that internal upheavals can't be switched on and off like a lightbulb. For better and worse, sad memories, fears, and anxieties are very much a part of who we are as human beings. They burn brightest in our minds at times we can't control—often sneaking up on us when we are least prepared to confront them. Sylvia Boorstein puts it this way:

The problem is that control doesn't work in the psychological arena, at least in the long run. The more we attempt to control our pain, the more we twist ourselves into knots and undermine our effectiveness.

Even without preplanning, the top ten of our psychological-emotional hit parade have a way of marching into the mind whenever there is a break in the clouds. As soon as space allows, the mind ruminates over memories or reflects about the future—mostly with remorse or apprehension.[16]

Not only can't we control our emotional distress, but recent research also shows that the struggle turns ordinary pain into intense suffering. The more determined we are to control our pain, the more the solution becomes the problem. Steven Hayes says

> The natural, rational thing to do when we face a problem is to figure out how to get rid of it and then actually get rid of it. In the external world, our ability to do just that is what allowed us to take over the planet. But that only works in the world outside the skin. . . . [S]uffering is so pervasive because our attempts at solving it only make it persist.[17]

Steven Hayes and Spencer Smith compare attempts at controlling psychological pain to trying to escape quicksand. The more we try to step out of it, the deeper we sink into it. In the psychological arena, counterintuitive as it might seem, the more we increase our determined efforts to escape our pain, the more we become ensnared.[18]

This trap of our own making can undermine our leadership as well as bring about other negative organizational consequences. For one thing, staying clear of situations that cause us pain means, in effect, staying clear of leadership opportunities. After all, learning is at the heart of leadership, and learning produces the pain of anxiety. We can't control the pain of leadership without avoiding leadership itself. For another, escaping pain can be like holding down the lid on a boiling cauldron: The effort requires unrelenting focus and energy and demands essential resources that should be devoted to doing our managerial work. In effect, choosing to control our pain means choosing to hold ourselves back from leading the way we want.

Attempts to control pain can also make us feel isolated and alone. We say to ourselves, "What's the matter with me? I shouldn't be in such pain. Other managers aren't in this kind of turmoil!" When such sentiments are a common experience, they can produce a conspiracy of silence. After all, we tell ourselves, it would be shameful to drop our masks and discuss how we truly feel. Moreover, constantly wearing a mask is like carrying a heavy weight. To always be "on," particularly when we think we must prove that we measure up, can create significant stress and anguish. It takes courage to break this pattern, as we saw in this chapter's opening vignette.

> *To always be "on," particularly when we think we must prove that we measure up, can create significant stress and anguish. It takes courage to break this pattern.*

Attempts at control can have additional negative organizational consequences. Controlling our pain can

- Lead to bad decisions. We take steps to get rid of complex problems quickly, sacrificing the time and attention these issues deserve;
- Undermine trust and credibility. Our staff intuitively knows that we must be confused, furious, or mortified; not to acknowledge these feelings at all makes us appear out of touch;
- Distance us from our colleagues. If our organization suffers a major loss, but we fail to acknowledge our anguish, we sacrifice the chance to develop strong relationships built on a common humanity.

Like it or not, the Measure Up Monster is real for many managers. We can't win a head-on battle with our MUM.

An Alternative: Acceptance and Change

In order to get unstuck, both in our minds and at our offices, we need to find a workable alternative to our battery-draining efforts to run away from pain. The familiar Serenity Prayer, attributed to theologian Reinhold Niebuhr, provides helpful guidance:

> God grant me the serenity to accept the things I cannot change,
>
> The courage to change the things I can,
>
> And the wisdom to know the difference.

We would be better leaders, I suggest, if we *accepted* our internal distress and focused our energies on *changing the world* in pursuit of our goals and values.[19]

In essence, acceptance means *welcoming* our painful thoughts and feelings—which indeed we cannot change—as part of who we are. To *welcome* pain, we must be willing to fully *experience* it, which is different from *wanting* it. Acceptance is a stance we take toward pain—the choice to embrace what we have thought of as the enemy, while letting go of our fight to control it.

Acceptance is not "nihilistic self-defeat; neither is it tolerating and putting up with your pain," say Hayes and Smith. "It is very, very different than that. Those heavy, sad, dark forms of 'acceptance' are almost the exact opposite of the active, vital embrace of the moment that we mean."[20]

"Paradoxically, the first step toward healthy emotional regulation," say Eifert and Forsyth, "is letting go of our attempts to control unwanted emotional experiences and accepting what we have for what it is; that is, to acknowledge the presence of fear, anxiety, worry, sadness, and anger."[21]

The core of this hard-to-fathom idea is illustrated by the familiar puzzle of the Chinese finger trap, where the goal is to free yourself after inserting your index fingers into each end of a woven bamboo tube. If you try to pull your fingers out straight and fast, the tube tightens. The more you struggle to escape, the more you are trapped. The trick is to first push your fingers in and then slide them out gently. The paradox of the Chinese finger trap is a metaphor for freeing ourselves to make choices by letting go of our internal drama. This is just the opposite of what we have been taught.[22]

How to let go of the struggle is also illustrated by what many of us learned at the seashore as children. How do we cope with ocean waves that threaten to engulf us in their headlong rush to break on the beach? Rather than running away or standing our ground, we've learned to avoid the slap and pull by diving into the darkest part of the wave, emerging on the other side in calmer water.

Now it is one thing to advise managers to dive into their dark wave and accept their pain; it is quite another thing for them to be able to heed this advice. After all, the stakes are very high, and the advice suggests the exact opposite of how we normally solve problems. And then there's MUM, of course, telling us that pain means failure and accepting will only confirm us as losers and quitters. Indeed, when I was a dean (and, I might add, a hardheaded manager), receiving such

Letting go takes both the recognition that old strategies haven't worked and the motivation needed to address the resulting struggle. It also takes a conscious choice to try something radically different.

advice felt as counterintuitive—and flaky—as shouting, "You have to let go!" to a frightened friend dangling by his fingertips from a sheer cliff. Letting go is a lot easier said than done.

To say the least, letting go takes both the recognition that old strategies haven't worked and the motivation needed to address the resulting struggle. It also takes a conscious choice to try something radically different. At bottom, it may require suspension of disbelief and the blind courage to risk falling into the void.

Replacing control with acceptance also takes practice. We need to become more aware of our experiences in the moment and learn to recognize that we are more than our fleeting thoughts and feelings.[23] Replacing our control habit with new skills also requires persistence—and the resilience to bounce back when our old habits rear their ugly heads once again. To help avoid relapses, you may want to create a device to focus your attention. One idea is to invent and invoke a personal mantra—something like "pain is not failure; it's only pain," or "acceptance is a sign of strength." What is important is that it works for you.

In addition to Hayes and Smith's "vital embrace," the proposed alternative spotlights the fact that even the most beneficial change is painful—and that leadership is inevitably about change. The idea is to switch our attention from controlling our pain to exploring what we want to accomplish as leaders. Then, and probably only then, can we effectively choose our direction and begin to change those things in our external world that can be changed. "It is about choosing to go forward in directions that are uniquely theirs," say Eifert and Forsyth, "*and* accepting what is inside them, what comes with them, and what accompanies them along the way."[24]

This, too, is a lot easier said than done. As the Serenity Prayer suggests, it takes courage to change. Indeed, it takes courage for managers to seek out what I call the "leadership zone"—that place on the boundary between what we know and don't know where the necessary work of learning new ways takes place. Putting ourselves into this zone of learning and leading is inevitably accompanied by feelings of anxiety and loss. It takes courage to work on this scary frontier, with all the doubts and fears of getting lost. It takes courage to hold steady in the midst of the unsettling uncertainty and conflict that mark organizational change. In short, it takes courage to choose to fully embrace change and all the pain it entails.[25]

To gain control on the leadership stage, first we must *give up* control of our behind-the-curtains drama. Next we must choose to change what we can, muster the courage to do it, and willingly take our pain along for the ride.

UNMASKING PAIN AT THE OFFICE

In addition to adopting a new agenda of acceptance and change, we face the challenge of how to handle our inner stuff at the office, where masking is the norm. I suggest that we *selectively* reveal our pain. While it may be futile to control the *experience* of emotional distress, it is possible to control its *expression.* Different roles—and different situations—appropriately call for different masks.

In many situations, of course, it is only sensible to avoid babbling about our emotional distress. To show our real feelings would undermine our authority and effectiveness, not to mention upset our colleagues. A good example comes from Katherine Graham, former chief of the *Washington Post,* who in her autobiography describes her fears about a possible strike by the newspaper's unions:

> I felt desperate and secretly wondered if I might have blown the whole thing and lost the paper. I didn't really see how we were going to manage. . . . Yet, despite my inner turmoil, I had to appear calm and determined and to come across as optimistic in order to convey that attitude to others.[26]

Stories like Graham's lead seasoned managers, in their rare quiet moments, to jokingly compare their life to that of a duck gliding across a pond. Above the water's surface, it's all grace and smooth sailing; underneath, it's nothing but frantic paddling to maintain momentum and direction.

In many situations, however, it makes sense to drop our masks at the office, at least partially. I'm not talking about revealing our darkest secrets or about pillow talk. Instead, I'm suggesting a third-level unmasking—that is, the revelation of the next level of feelings that we might not normally disclose.

Another prominent figure, Rudy Giuliani, provides a helpful example. He received lavish praise for his handling of the 9/11 disaster in New York City—not only for displaying the kind of calm that Graham described above, but also for revealing his feelings for those who had died. "The number of casualties will be more than any of us can bear ultimately," he responded to a reporter's question at his first 9/11 news conference.[27] By showing his compassion, he demonstrated the importance of genuine signs of anguish and caring, particularly in moments of trauma.

But pain does not come only in the form of catastrophic loss. I have already cited Schein's writings about learning anxiety, and noted that much of what we think of as the day-to-day work of leadership is about getting ourselves and others to learn new ways of being and behaving and to put them into effect. Schein argues that, in order to achieve change, leaders must reveal their own anxiety in dealing with change:

> [U]nless leaders become learners themselves—unless they can acknowledge their own vulnerabilities and uncertainties—then transformational learning will never take place. When leaders become genuine learners, they set a good example and help to create a psychologically safe environment for others.[28]

An inevitable by-product of learning is confusion, which Barry Jentz and I suggest is widespread among managers. We argue that managers need to embrace their confusion and the pain associated with it—and, rather than hiding it, go public by asserting the struggle that can be involved in learning and making sense of new and unfamiliar situations. Doing so, we think, "helps others to do the same—to claim their own confusion and begin trying to make sense out of a disorienting situation. By taking the lead, you make it easy for others to follow."[29]

Another example comes from my opening vignette about the superintendent who wakes up crying. We can almost feel the relief in the room as a respected colleague breaks the taboo against self-disclosure by making himself vulnerable. We can almost hear each of the other superintendents say, "You mean I'm not alone?"

This story has added value as a reminder that how and to whom we reveal our emotions can be crucial. In many cases, unmasking only works in the presence of the right audience. As dean, I once gave a speech to a group of donors and faculty members in which I likened fund-raising to building friendships. While telling stories about several donors in the audience, I became visibly choked up. The donors, with whom I had developed strong bonds of trust, told me later that they were deeply moved by my remarks. In contrast, several worried faculty members thought I had lost my marbles, misreading my tears as a sign of affliction, not affection.

Instead of *showing* our feelings—instead of acting out—we can describe them with precision and candor. Such behavior is the very opposite of losing control, but it is still a constructive form of letting go. For example, the superintendent in the opening vignette didn't burst into tears; instead, he let people know some of the details of his sleepless nights. Or we can put a name to our pain, perhaps by saying something like, "When you changed the decision after our staff meeting this morning, I was very upset because it undermines my authority with my staff," rather than venting our feelings by ranting and raving.

Indeed, how we deliver our message is just as important as our words. In our research on confusion, Jentz and I concluded that "unless you unambiguously assert, with conviction and without apology, your sense of being confused, others will fulfill your worst expectations—concluding that you *are* weak—and they will be less willing to engage in a shared process of interpersonal learning."[30]

In the end, it is next to impossible to successfully assert our troubling feelings unless we accept

> *Instead of showing our feelings—instead of acting out—we can describe them with precision and candor.*

them as a legitimate part of who we are in that moment. "Unless you come to recognize that being confused is a normal—even necessary—consequence of leadership," Jentz and I suggest, "it will be difficult for you to state firmly that you are at a loss."[31] In other words, it is hard to reveal what we don't embrace.

On the whole, managers are quite wary about revealing their inner turmoil—their uncertainty and pain. And when they do decide to disclose, I'm guessing that they don't come close to my proposed third-level unmasking. There are good reasons for this reluctance: disclosure violates norms; there are few guideposts as to when, where, and how to reveal; and surely disclosure is sometimes counterproductive.

Nonetheless, I think managers should experiment with being more revealing, perhaps starting with their closest colleagues and pacing their disclosures so that common customs are not challenged too quickly. In many cases, disarming honesty about our inner life, shared in the correct way within the correct context, can lead to stronger connections and better problem solving—and to an energizing sense of common humanity, the sense that we are all in this together.

IT's NOT REALLY ABOUT THE PAIN

In this chapter, I've speculated about the taboo topic of leadership-related pain in the hope of stimulating research and of supporting practitioners in their efforts to deal with their pain. These musings rest on the view that leadership can be extremely rewarding and exhilarating, but that pain is certainly part of the work. As Benjamin Franklin once said, there is "no gain without pain."[32]

Drawing on the rich work of others and on my own experiences, I've suggested that emotional pain is a normal part of life, and it's only human to try to resolve our personal dramas through the same approach we have found effective in solving external problems: exercising control. Research and everyday experience suggest, however, that this common approach can backfire and create a bigger problem: intense internal suffering as we struggle to control, suppress, or evade an essential part of who we are.

The more we try to control and hide, the more we can sap our energy, eat our time, and divert our attention from what we really want.

I've also hypothesized that the demands and expectations of leadership can amplify the normal pains of living, and that enduring misconceptions about the superhuman requirements of leadership can amplify the ordinary human predisposition to control pain. As a consequence, some managers—what percentage I do not know—go to great lengths to control and hide their abundant pain because it internally signals that we don't measure up as leaders.

In the process, we add fear of failure to our original pain, which creates an even bigger problem. The more we try to control and hide, the more we can sap our energy, eat our time, and divert our attention from what we really want. In this sense, I am not writing about the pain, but rather about the negative consequences of attempting to control the fear of failure as a leader.

In the end, I did not mean for this chapter to be simply a somber look at the high costs of leadership. It's not really about the pain, or about the fear of failing to measure up. Rather, this chapter is about taking an honest—and optimistic—look at ourselves as leaders and at our willingness to change. It's about having the courage to release ourselves to pursue our dreams. It's about taking a new look at pain and embracing this deep and age-old enemy as a necessary—and even welcome—companion. Ultimately, it's about moving forward on our journey—in work, in life, and in leadership.

NOTES

1. This is the gist of a story I heard while teaching a seminar for school superintendents at the Penn Graduate School of Education on April 12, 2006.

2. Much of what follows draws heavily from the growing body of literature on Acceptance and Commitment Therapy (ACT). I have tried to adapt these ideas and apply them in a nontherapeutic way to thinking about leadership. The book that I've drawn from the most, both in the ideas presented and in the chapter's organization, is *Acceptance and Commitment Therapy for Anxiety Disorders,* by Georg H. Eifert and John P. Forsyth (Oakland, CA: New Harbinger, 2005). For a discussion of ACT aimed at a lay audience, also see *Get Out of Your Mind and Into Your Life* by Steven C. Hayes with Spencer Smith (Oakland, CA: New Harbinger, 2005). On the subject of Buddhism, my favorite book is *Don't Just Do Something, Sit There* by Sylvia Boorstein (New York: HarperCollins, 1996), which provides an engaging introduction to the practice of mindfulness. Also see *Buddhism Without Beliefs* by Stephen Batchelor (New York: Riverhead Books, 1997). On the subject of military strategy, no one can compare with Carl von Clausewitz, who has written about the dangers of leadership and the fog of war—and what it takes to be a successful commander. For a volume that makes Clausewitz's ideas come alive in a nonmilitary setting, see *Clausewitz on Strategy,* edited by Tiha von Ghyczy et al. (New York: Wiley, 2001). On the subject of leadership, see *Leadership on the Line* by Ronald A. Heifetz and Marty Linsky (Boston: Harvard Business School Press, 2002) and Barry Jentz and Jerome T. Murphy, "Embracing Confusion: What Leaders Do When They Don't Know What To Do" (*Phi Delta Kappan,* January 2005).

3. Barry Jentz acted as my extraordinarily able consultant for many years.

4. Hill, L. (2003). *Becoming a manager* (pp. 175–176). Boston: Harvard Business School Press.

5. Ibid., pp. 178–189.

6. Coutu, D. L. (2002, April 15). The darker side of organizational learning. An interview with Edgar H. Schein. *Working Knowledge Newsletter,* p. 1. Boston: Harvard Business School. Available: http://hbswk .hbs.edu/archive/2888.html

7. Heifetz, R. A., & Linsky, M. (2002, June). A survival guide for leaders. *Harvard Business Review,* p. 5.

8. Ibid., p. 6.

9. Ibid., p. 12.

10. Hill, L. (2003).

11. And of course, there is always denial—we simply refuse to admit to ourselves that we are feeling the emotional distress of leading. We may say to ourselves, I'm not hurting from the criticism, ashamed of my stupid remarks, or sad about losing my colleagues as friends. Not me.

12. Personal correspondence, July 10, 2006.

13. Eifert & Forsyth (2005), p. 63.

14. Roberts is at court's helm, but he isn't yet in control. (2006, July 2). *New York Times,* p. 1.

15. The ACT literature often refers to monsters, but I believe MUM is an original adaptation.

16. Boorstein (1996), p. 59.

17. Interview with Steven Hayes by New Harbinger (2004). Available: http://www.newharbinger.com/client/client_pages/monthinterview_ HAYES.cfmp

18. Hayes & Smith (2005), pp. 3–4.

19. This focus on acceptance and change is at the heart of the ACT literature. Also see the Heifetz and Linsky article (2002), p. 11, for other approaches to dealing with the pain of leadership, such as establishing a safe place to reflect, finding a confidante, and distinguishing between role and self.

20. Hayes & Smith (2005), p. 7.

21. Eifert & Forsyth (2005), p. 53.

22. The Chinese finger trap is widely used as a metaphor in the ACT literature. For example, see Eifert & Forsyth (2005), pp. 146–149.

23. The ACT literature stresses the practice of such techniques as "defusion" and mindfulness. See, for example, Hayes & Smith (2005). Also, see the literature on Buddhism, such as Boorstein (1996), on meditation and the practice of mindfulness.

24. Eifert & Forsyth (2005), p. 7.

25. In his classic study of war, Clausewitz argues that courage is the most important quality of warriors as they face the danger and uncertainty of battle. See von Ghyczy (2001), p. 56.

26. Cited in Badaracco, J. L. (2006). *Questions of character* (p. 110). Boston: Harvard Business School Press.

27. *Rudy Giuliani: The man and his moment.* (2002). Teaching Case No. 1681.2. Kennedy School of Government, Harvard University. Available: http://www.ksgcase.harvard.edu

28. Coutu (2002), p. 2.

29. Jentz & Murphy (2005), p. 363.

30. Ibid., p. 363.

31. Ibid., p. 363.

32. *Poor Richard's Almanac.*

INDEX

The Corwin Press logo—a raven striding across an open book—represents the union of courage and learning. Corwin Press is committed to improving education for all learners by publishing books and other professional development resources for those serving the field of PreK–12 education. By providing practical, hands-on materials, Corwin Press continues to carry out the promise of its motto: **"Helping Educators Do Their Work Better."**

The HOPE Foundation logo stands for Harnessing Optimism and Potential Through Education. The HOPE Foundation helps to develop and support educational leaders over time at district- and state-wide levels to create school cultures that sustain all students' achievement, especially low-performing students.

NSDC's mission is to ensure success for all students by serving as the international network for those who improve schools and by advancing individual and organization development.